Teaching History with Musicals

Teaching History with . . . Series

Series Editor: Cynthia J. Miller

Teaching History with Musicals, by Kathryn Edney, 2017.
Teaching History with Newsreels and Public Service Shorts, by Aaron Gulyas, 2017.
Teaching History with Science Fiction Films, by A. Bowdoin Van Riper, 2017.

Teaching History with Musicals

Kathryn Edney

ROWMAN & LITTLEFIELD
Lanham • Boulder • New York • London

Published by Rowman & Littlefield
A wholly owned subsidary of The Rowman & Littlefield Publishing Group, Inc.
4501 Forbes Boulevard, Suite 200, Lanham, Maryland 20706
www.rowman.com

Unit A, Whitacre Mews, 26-34 Stannary Street, London SE11 4AB

British Library Cataloguing in Publication Information Available

Library of Congress Cataloging-in-Publication Data Available

ISBN 9781442278424 (pbk. : alk. paper) | ISBN 9781442278431 (electronic)

∞ ™ The paper used in this publication meets the minimum requirements of American National Standard for Information Sciences Permanence of Paper for Printed Library Materials, ANSI/NISO Z39.48-1992.

Printed in the United States of America

Contents

Acknowledgments

I owe series editor Cynthia Miller so many thanks for the opportunity to write this book. She has been nothing but kind and patient with me as I navigated the process. Thanks must also go to the Regis College Faculty Development Committee for awarding me a Kaneb Faculty Development Grant during the 2014–2015 academic year. Mrs. Virginia Kaneb and her family are very generous for providing this kind of funding for research and scholarship. My final thanks must go to Dr. Penny Glynn, former dean of the School of Nursing and Health Sciences at Regis College. Unsolicited, she reached across disciplinary boundaries and offered to read early chapter drafts. She knew when I needed help before I knew to ask for it, and I am profoundly grateful for her advice, support, and friendship.

Introduction

As Tom Gunning noted in "The Whole Town's Gawking," film musicals adhere to an older form of film aesthetic: the cinema of attraction.[1] The narrative drive of the film is paused for the actors to break out into a purely performative mode that calls attention to itself; indeed, in many film musicals the actors pause and hold their poses after singing and dancing for the audience applause that never comes. While science-fiction and horror films have similar moments of pure spectacle, it is still the case that for a film musical, the musical moments that define it also operate against many of the defining characteristics of mainstream narrative cinema in ways that do not occur in other genres.[2] It is perhaps for this reason that film musicals typically divide audiences. There are those who cannot accept the musical disruptions and those who embrace such narrative lapses.[3]

The fantastical, utopian elements of film musicals and their comparative lack of narrative integrity when placed against other films would seem to make them difficult texts to use within history courses for two reasons. First, whether the methodology used by a historian is world-systems theory or microhistory, the goal is to make sense of the past. Although postmodernism emphasizes fragmentation and discontinuities, the prevailing mode through which historians make sense of, and teach about, the past involves narrative. While many theorists have debated the value of narrative and history, and the ways in which standard narrative tropes subconsciously shape the kind of history that is told, breaking completely free from the story-based model of a beginning, a middle, and an end when relating a historical event or exploring a person's biography is not easy.[4] And as public historian Marianne Babal argues in her essay about "sticky history," one way to combat the "I hate history" attitude articulated by many nonhistorians is to embrace the narrative mode and establish emotional connections between the past and the present.[5] Musical films, with the distancing effect song and dance often provokes, and the fragmented mode of storytelling embraced by the genre, thus arguably run counter to the overall ethos of history as a discipline.

The second apparent obstacle to using the film musical as a lens through which to understand history and historical thinking is the very fantastical, nonrealistic nature of the genre. History, as so many undergraduates like to state, is about facts and about articulating "what really happened." Even a musical film grounded in historical research such as *1776* cannot get around the fact that Benjamin Franklin did not sing about the ways in which the colonies were coming together as a new nation. Film musicals may be set in the past or deal with real events of history, but it is difficult to argue that such films engage with history in ways that are in keeping with the historical record, or even that they are in keeping with the ways in which real people behave over the course of their daily lives.

Given the above objections, why does this book even exist? Why make the attempt to teach history using film musicals as source texts? As Alan Marcus and colleagues have observed in *Teaching History with Film*, while movies are a very common teaching tool in the history classroom, "history films" based on "real-life events" are often viewed as exceedingly problematic to use without an extensive amount of scaffolding for students. Films purporting to be factually accurate are nonetheless heavily fictionalized and dramatized for narrative effect. It can be difficult for students to parse out the differences between representations of reality and the historical realities when films are working very hard to erase those differences. Contemporary films about the past are also embedded within current political and social concerns, and thus can have the effect of encouraging a passive presentism among students, reinforcing the misconception that "people in the past were just like us, only dressed differently."[6]

However, this book argues that the very nature of film musicals as discussed above can serve as an antidote to the problematics of using films within the classroom. The "cinema of attraction" mode of address disrupts the narrative, which prevents complete absorption into the world as represented on the screen. There is less risk of students conflating how a film musical represents historical realities with the historical realities themselves. Further, it becomes difficult for students to be passive watchers of what occurs on the screen given the shifts that occur in musicals between the forward momentum of the plot and the interruptions (song and dance) of that momentum necessitated by the genre's conventions. Such distance allows for the development of interpretative skills and can open up discussions about the nature of "doing history" and the constructed nature of all history writing. When used carefully, musical films about a historical event or person can also transmit and reinforce content, as well as skills, in historical methodologies and thinking.

In the first chapter, a brief history of the American film musical is sketched out, with particular attention paid to the major benchmarks and conventions of the genre. Chapter 2 ("Historical Concepts") engages in a series of case studies to focus on particular issues in teaching historical thinking and content. Chapter 3 focuses on the ways in which film musicals can be used to teach the history of the United States within the context of the survey course, while the final chapter fills a similar function regarding the teaching of Western civilization.

It must be noted that musical films are also an excellent means for embedding discussions of gender, race, class, and, crucially, how those various categories intersect. Within a survey history course, incorporating the concept of intersectionality can be a daunting task within the larger frame of moving through important dates and events. However, as the connections and tensions between the women's suffrage and the abolitionist movements in the United States prove, while twentieth-century feminists coined the term *intersectionality*, historically women and men have long negotiated multiple social, political, and cultural boundaries as ascribed to them.[7] In part, because the basic form of musicals is so rigid, the intersections among the different social categories occupied by a film's characters can be more easily discerned. Therefore, throughout the book assignments and discussion questions related to intersectionality, as well as more focused questions regarding race, class, and gender, will be referenced.[8]

* * *

Musical films as a genre are not perfect vehicles for teaching straightforward, fact-based historical content. The genre as a whole tends toward nostalgia and fantasy; the convention of including song and dance necessarily requires that nonmusical information is compressed or overlooked; and if one is looking for a musical film for each significant period in history there will be disappointment. However, if musical films are used as a mode of opening up discussions regarding the nature of doing history and thinking historically, then their value as teaching tools can be more fully realized. The elements that seemingly make the musical film as a genre problematic when used within a history classroom can be reframed as advantages. Students, especially those at the college level, can be placed in the position of actively engaging in historical knowledge in order to compensate for the flawed ways in which musicals represent history.

Even backstage musicals, which provide a logical excuse for why its characters insist on breaking out into song and dance, ultimately do not pretend to be realistic. Unlike a documentary, musicals acknowledge that they represent a peculiar construction of the world, a world where song and dance naturally occurs, but of course such occurrences are not natural at all.

The same type of ethos holds true for creating historical meaning, crafting historical narratives, and asking questions of the past. No matter how students might seek to naturalize why the American colonies defeated England during the American Revolution, the outcome was not certain. Canada's history with England is certainly proof of how the story of the United States might have gone differently. The musical *1776*, however, is an even better reminder of the constructed nature of historical knowledge and of the ways in which historians attempt to make sense of past events.

Musical films are also very useful in the classroom when discussing ethnicity, race, gender, sexuality, and class as historical constructs. The film *Flower Drum Song* (1961) is set in then-contemporary Chinatown, San Francisco. The film contains its Chinese and Chinese American characters within a limited geographic setting and includes a song ("Chop Suey") about the process of assimilation and the nature of a hyphenated identity. A few crowd scenes aside, there are no other races or ethnicities represented within the movie. An obvious choice in teaching a course about the history of race/ethnicity in the United States would be to screen this film alongside *West Side Story* (1961) and to consider how the representations of Puerto Ricans, whites, and Asians are variously constructed, and how those representations connect to the history of immigration patterns and policies in the United States.

However, both musicals are perhaps more famous for individual songs about gender than they are for songs about ethnicity. *Flower Drum Song* contains "I Enjoy Being a Girl," which star Nancy Kwan as "Linda" sings in front of a mirror; it is a complicated anthem to femininity and the way in which women perform the feminine for themselves and for others. This latter song makes no reference to Linda's ethnicity. For its part, *West Side Story* features "I Feel Pretty," also, coincidentally—or not so coincidentally, performed in front of a mirror. Both films are very much embedded in the cultural moment of the 1960s and provide multiple ways through which theories of gender, and the history of women in the United States, can be discussed.

Flower Drum Song and *West Side Story* might also be used in a course on the history of class and labor in the United States. The former film links together education and class, and the proper types of labor for men and for women, and extols the virtues of conspicuous consumption. The latter implicitly addresses unemployment, examines how race/ethnicity impacts perceptions of class, and questions the applicability of the American Dream and class mobility. Finally, of course, both films could also be used in a survey course about the history of immigration or a survey course that wishes to focus on the early 1960s before it became known as a decade dominated by hippies and the antiwar movement.

Both *Flower Drum Song* and *West Side Story* tell relatively simple, for-mulaic heterosexual love stories, and yet in execution, the very formula of the musical provides the means through which historical attitudes are embed-ded for students to unpack. Both films are "about" issues of ethnicity, and yet as many scholars have noted, varying ideas concerning gender are paramount to both films. A film such as *Top Hat*, which features no actors of color, can nonetheless engage with questions of race through its absence. While the clear focus of *Top Hat* is, unsurprisingly, on gender—Rick Altman's theory on the ways in which musical films are structured makes that focus clear—representations of class and labor are threaded throughout. In other words, within the context of more topic-oriented courses in history, the content of these films can be used to explore any number of relevant themes. Further, the production histories of the films provide another means through which the histories of class, race, and gender can be studied and better understood.

As stated throughout this book, using musical films as the vehicle through which to teach history means that any instructor will need to adjust for holes in the historical content. However, as a genre, film musicals are an excellent means through which to teach students about the nature of historical knowl-edge and the ways in which historians think and write about the past.

NOTES

1. Tom Gunning, "The Whole Town's Gawking: Early Cinema and the Visual Experience of Modernity," *Yale Journal of Criticism* 7, no. 2 (1994): 189–201.

2. It is important to note that in her book on film pornography, Linda Williams notes some of the similarities between the structures of pornography and the structures of musical films. See the chapter "Generic Pleasures" in particular. Linda Williams, *Hard Core: Power, Pleas-ure, and the "Frenzy of the Visible"* (Berkeley: University of California Press, 1999).

3. Richard Dyer, "Entertainment and Utopia," in *Only Entertainment*, 19–35 (New York: Routledge, 1999).

4. Hayden White, "The Historical Text as Literary Artifact," in *Tropics of Discourse: Essays in Cultural Criticism*, 81–100 (Baltimore: Johns Hopkins University Press, 1985).

5. Marianne Babal, "Sticky History: Connecting Historians with the Public," *Public Histo-rian* 32, no. 4 (Fall 2010): 76–84.

6. Although their book does not address higher education, their ideas on using film in the classroom are broadly applicable: Alan S. Marcus, Scott Alan Metzger, Richard J. Paxton, and Jeremy D. Stoddard, *Teaching History with Film: Strategies for Secondary Social Studies* (New York: Routledge, 2010).

7. Avtar Brah and Ann Phoenix, "Ain't I a Woman? Revisiting Intersectionality," *Journal of International Women's Studies* 5, no. 3 (May 2004): 75–86, http://vc.bridgew.edu/.

8. For history topic courses with a particular thematic focus on race or gender, the majority of the films referenced in this book could be used to highlight historical practices, social attitudes, or both.

CONCEPTS

Chapter One

A Short History of Musical Films

For those familiar with the history of American film musicals, this chapter may well be superfluous; however, for those with more limited knowledge, this chapter provides a grounding in the key historical benchmarks, people, and studios involved in musical films. The history is chronological in scope by decade, with the understanding that many stars and studios straddle and cross those decades; the periodization is not perfect. In addition, the basic genre conventions of the form, and how those conventions shaped the history of the genre, are discussed. Musicals have their own particular grammar and language, and for teaching purposes, it is important to have a solid understanding of how and why musicals construct filmic worlds in which singing and dancing as a mode of expression is natural and normal.[1]

While certainly other genre films can be recognized as such because they recycle particular themes and narrative devices,[2] from its beginnings in 1927 with *The Jazz Singer*, the film musical seemingly recycled everything: older forms of entertainment (vaudeville and revues), songs and tunes (all but two of the songs in *Singin' in the Rain* originated in other films), and narrative structures, actors, and themes. As a mode of popular entertainment, musicals as a genre constantly look backward and reflect on the past. While those reflections are more often than not nostalgic—a longing for a past that did not really exist—the awareness of the past manifested by musicals can help students be more aware of how they characterize the past as well.

One of the key genre attributes of the film musical is the different ways in which various films attempt to solve the "problem" of singing (and dancing) within the narrative. In particular, a clear tension exists between the forward momentum of the plot and the musical numbers arresting that forward momentum.[3] As will be discussed below, the easiest way for musicals to address their performativity is to set the narrative within the context of a theater or

3

other live-performance contexts. That is, many musical films, including *The Jazz Singer*, fall within the category of the "backstage" or "putting on a show" musical. However, there are other methods of addressing the place of song and dance. For example, 2002's *Chicago* places the musical numbers within the mind of the protagonists; the singing and dancing taking place is a fantastical inner monologue that no one else can see or experience. Fantasy-based or fairy-tale musicals, such as *The Wiz* (1978), capitalize on a narrative world that is constructed to be nonrealistic. Thus, music or magic is equally plausible within the framework of the film. Finally, folk musicals, such as *Oklahoma!* create narratives where its characters "naturally" sing as an expression of their community and culture.[4]

In his classic exploration of the film musical genre, Rick Altman proposed that another way in which film musicals address the tension between plot and music is through parallel, rather than linear, constructions rooted in the differences between the male and female leads.[5] While Hollywood films in general emphasize cause and effect in the plot—the man does something terrible, so the woman retaliates—musicals are designed differently. For example, in one scene, a man is shown singing in a bar. In the next scene, a woman is shown singing at home. The first action did not cause the second. Rather, the two parallel scenes set up a relationship between the two characters. First, the sequence illustrates that the man and the woman are alike. They both express themselves through song and are therefore a plausible romantic couple. Second, the two scenes highlight the romantic obstacle or difference to be overcome in the remainder of the film: he is outgoing; she is shy. How that obstacle will be resolved—will the two somehow meet in the middle, will he become less of a braggart, or might she transform into a nightclub singer?—is part of the larger patterns within the genre.[6]

The history of the musical film genre is not smooth, nor is it easy to characterize; it can therefore also serve as an important object lesson to students about the messiness of history itself.[7] While it can often seem to students as though America was "destined" to win the Revolutionary War because we know the outcome, no such trajectory is readily apparent in the history of film musicals. As Richard Barrios notes, "Where other genres simply pass in and out of style, musicals soar and careen and nosedive."[8] Throughout this chapter, although many of the typical benchmarks—for instance, Fred and Ginger, and the Freed Unit—will be addressed, other, less standard markers—such as cowboy musicals and Annette Funicello and Frankie Avalon—will also be discussed as a way to mark the idiosyncratic nature of the history, and the nature, of the genre. Such an approach should also allow faculty to think through the different kinds of musicals not mentioned in this book that might be included within the classroom by thinking both within, and outside, canonical works.

In terms of social history, it is also important to note that alongside the many Hollywood films being produced, a "separate but equal" film production, distribution, and screening system existed for African American filmmakers and audiences. From the 1910s through the mid-1950s, independent black-run studios and filmmakers produced all-black movies for black audiences that white audiences never saw, much less knew existed. This aspect of the history of film in America is important to highlight to students, as it is important to explore why, how, and when African Americans were incorporated within musicals meant for white audiences. To help ensure that the African American presence and influence within the history of musical films are not lost, African American–made films meant for African American audiences and Hollywood-produced musicals with all-black casts will be woven throughout this chapter rather than addressed as a separate issue. [9]

CLASSROOM DISCUSSION STARTERS

Questions pertaining to the history and genre conventions of film musicals are an important means through which historical thinking can be modeled for students. They can also ease the way into discussing the films in terms of specific historical content or methodologies. The questions below are deliberately broad.

- Within the context of the film's narrative, what purpose did the production number serve?
- In what ways do the styles of music (and dance) used in the film help to define the characters, the historical period, and the place?
- What "givens" (in terms of race, gender, sexuality, class, etc.) are in operation within the film's narrative? Why might that be the case?
- What types of people are missing from this film, in terms of both race/ethnicity and sexual preference, and what types of professions are missing? Why might this be the case?
- Would this film be coherent and understandable without the song-and-dance numbers? Why or why not?
- What type/subgenre of musical film is this? Does the subgenre matter, and if so, how?
- Why might this film be considered "canonical" (or as falling outside of the canon) within the history of film musicals? Do you agree with the received wisdom concerning the film?
- Many scholars view film musicals as a distinctly "American" genre. In what ways is this film engaging with, or performing, an idea about America or American-ness?

- In what ways is this film in conversation with other films we have viewed this semester?
- Are there patterns to the ways in which musical films depict history? If so, what are they, and why might these patterns matter?

THE 1920s AND 1930s

For all that it is popularly known as the first "talkie," *The Jazz Singer* is a predominantly silent film with several crucial scenes synced with sound.[10] It might therefore more properly be referred to as a "protomusical," rather than as a fully developed musical film. However, the film does incorporate many of the tropes and conventions that came to characterize backstage musicals. It emphasizes performance, and star Al Jolson reveals the behind-the-scenes processes that occur before and after a star does his turn on the stage. While in terms of musicality and choreography *The Jazz Singer* is no *Cabaret* (1972), the latter can nonetheless trace its roots back to the former.[11]

The first full-blown musical that called itself a musical, and that would be more recognizable to students as fitting the criteria for a musical, was 1929's *Broadway Melody*. Produced by MGM, its legendary slogan "All Talking! All Singing! All Dancing!" proclaimed how sound changed film. It also firmly established the now well-known conventions for the backstage/"putting on a show" subgenre of musical films. Its descendants from 1933's *42nd Street* to 2002's *8 Mile* follow or subvert the conventions, including a rising young star, rehearsals, and theater-as-community. From *Broadway Melody* then came a host of imitators, with a few standouts, particularly *42nd Street*.[12]

Another important landmark of 1929 is the all-black musical directed by King Vidor: *Hallelujah*. Similar to how African Americans were then being represented on the Broadway stage, the film depicts the life of a rural, Southern black family with a special emphasis on religious beliefs and practices. Given the intersections between religion and music in African American life, the emphasis on religion in films representing black life in rural America allowed for the "natural" use of music in these films. Altman would therefore characterize such films as "folk musicals," although clearly the racial politics behind, and on, the screen are more complex than such a term implies.[13]

Mainstream musical films of the 1930s were tied to the studio system, and the Warner Bros. studio in particular.[14] With the Great Depression and President Franklin Roosevelt's emphasis on the collective responsibility of American citizens to help raise the United States out of economic turmoil as context, Warner Bros. musicals unsurprisingly emphasized group cooperation as the means for achieving (theatrical) success. While director and choreographer Busby Berkeley is lauded for the complex geometry of his choreography, it should be noted that his massive, precise formations are impressive in part because of the sheer number of people working together to create a beautiful whole. The apparent star is, to a certain extent, the least important person in those films.[15]

A serious rival to Warner Bros. for audiences of musicals was RKO and that studio's pairing of Fred Astaire and Ginger Rogers; during the 1930s they made nine films together. Unlike the backstage musicals of Warner Bros., the Astaire-Rogers films emphasized light romance and "boy-meets-girl/boy-loses-girl/boy-gets-girl" story lines that privileged the stars over everyone else. While the plots varied little, songs by expert composers George Gershwin or Irving Berlin, choreography by Astaire and collaborator Hermes Pan, and generally witty scripts, provided many variations on how the plots were implemented. The RKO films of Astaire and Rogers also differed from the Berkeley films at Warner Bros. in terms of technique. The often-phantasmagorical choreography of Berkeley, coupled with his emphasis on female body parts, required close-ups and frequent editing. In contrast to Berkeley, and to capture his choreography in full, Astaire preferred long, unedited takes with his and his partner's bodies fully in the frame.[16] But for all of the differences between the styles of RKO and Warner Bros. productions, the musical comedies generated from these studios were firmly set in the contemporary world of the 1930s.

The other famous musical film couple from the 1930s was Nelson Eddy and Jeanette MacDonald, who starred in a series of eight operettas for MGM, including *Naughty Marietta* (1935) and *Rose Marie* (1936).[17] Like the Astaire/Rogers films, the Eddy/MacDonald films were primarily light romances, but one of the defining characteristics of an operetta is that it is set outside of contemporary life. Unlike Astaire/Rogers films or the Berkeley spectaculars, films featuring Eddy and MacDonald were typically set in the past or in exotic locations where the modern concerns of the Great Depression would not touch them.[18]

Alongside the Warner Bros. and RKO's live-action musicals were the animated musical shorts from Walt Disney known as the *Silly Symphonies* (1929–1939). The films, typically only a few minutes in length, are often not included in histories of the film musical; Mickey Mouse seemingly has little in common with Fred Astaire. Disney allowed his animators at the time the chance to experiment with different techniques and styles with an eye toward full-length animated films, and so the *Silly Symphonies* seem to fall outside of many of the established conventions of musical films. But shorts such as *Three Little Pigs* (1933) and its famous "Whose Afraid of the Big Bad Wolf?" were a significant part of the aural landscape on the United States, and the legacy of the *Silly Symphonies* continues in contemporary animated films such as *Frozen* (2013). Musicals create a fantasy world where song and dance is a normal part of self-expression. The extra layer of fantasy provided by animation should not distract from the point that animated musicals are still musicals, and the relatively short length of animated musicals can make screening them in the classroom less time consuming than feature films. [19]

It is also important to remember that while Warner Bros. and RKO produced many film musicals during the late 1920s through the 1930s, with a distinctive style attributable to each studio, MGM and other studios were also producing musicals, many of which have entered the musical film canon. For example, *The Wizard of Oz*, released in 1939 by MGM and produced by Arthur Freed, is a highly regarded classic that does not fall into either the backstage musical or the romantic comedy musical categories; with its focus on family, community, memory, and place, it straddles the subgenres Altman identified as "the fairytale musical" and "the folk musical."[20]

Throughout the 1930s and 1940s, and at the opposite end of the spectacle and glamor spectrums, small-scale studios such as Monogram Pictures, Republic Studios, and Grand National Pictures churned out films featuring singing cowboys—Gene Autry and Roy Rogers are the most well known—who could rope cattle, romance the girl, save the ranch, and sing a ballad while riding a horse. Artistically, such films may not have much merit, but they are nonetheless an interesting part of popular culture that is too often ignored when considering the history of film musicals.[21] Even African American producers jumped onto the singing cowboy craze with films like 1939's *The Bronze Buckaroo*, featuring jazz singer Herb Jeffries as cowboy Bob Blake. As sophisticated as the films of Astaire and Rogers are, they form only a small part of the wide array of musicals available to audiences, and a film such as *Tumbling Tumbleweeds* (1935) can be just as useful in the classroom as *Top Hat* when the goal is an exploration of American social history.

THE 1940s

By the 1940s significant advances had been made in film technology; everything from sound recording and lighting to the use of color. However, it would take until after the end of World War II for those technologies to be fully utilized. During the war, numerous black-and-white "canteen musicals" from different studios were released, including *Star-Spangled Rhythm* (1942), *Thank Your Lucky Stars* (1943), and *Hollywood Canteen* (1944). These musicals were often structured in the style of a variety show, with perhaps a thin thematic thread connecting a series of performances. Meant to entertain the troops and serve as pro-Ally propaganda, wartime films are an excellent way to familiarize students with the popular songs of the 1940s and with popular depictions of how audiences were supposed to view the war effort.[22]

It is important to remember, however, that not all "wartime musicals" were explicitly about World War II. Indeed, many musicals produced during the war were set in an idyllic prewar era and, like many of the Depression-era films before them, were meant to distract audiences from the realities of historical events.[23] One excellent example of a mainstream wartime film that glossed over the war is 1943's all-black-cast *Stormy Weather*, featuring Lena Horne and a host of famous black performers, including Bill Robinson, Cab Calloway, and Katherine Dunham. Released by 20th Century Fox, the film was a jazz-filled, "backstage musical" showcase.[24]

Toward the end of the war, another iteration of the musical, this time as envisioned by Arthur Freed at MGM Studios through the so-called Freed Unit–produced films, came to the fore. Among those musicals produced by Freed now considered to be synonymous with the genre itself are *On the Town* (1949), *An American in Paris* (1951), *Singin' in the Rain* (1952), and *The Band Wagon* (1953). The Freed Unit also produced the all-black-cast musical *Cabin in the Sky* (1943), which, like 1929's *Hallelujah*, focused on rural, Southern, religious black life.

The Freed Unit films, many of which featured iconic performances by Judy Garland or Gene Kelly, and directed by legends Vincente Minnelli or Stanley Donen, explicitly focused on naturalizing and integrating song, dance, and story together with a visual opulence often enhanced by the use of Technicolor film.[25] The Freed Unit musicals all have a very similar "look" to them, and the ways in which the narratives shift from dialogue to song and back again are portrayed as normal parts of the everyday lives of the characters. But as much as Freed viewed integration—in the formal, if not the racial, sense—as an important artistic statement for his films, it must be remembered that other filmmakers eschewed the integration of elements in their movies.[26] Fragmentation and integration in movie musicals existed alongside each other, and it cannot be said that the latter evolved into the former.

The postwar era also witnessed a change in dancing styles, with the elegant Fred Astaire giving way to the rougher Gene Kelly.[27] Both men were equally skilled, but where Astaire's tap styles emphasized a sense of effortlessness and elegance, Kelly's tap styles were more muscular, inviting audiences to marvel at his physical strength and gymnastic ability.[28] In part, these changes were the result of cultural shifts: after World War II ideas about masculinity shifted, and men who danced could connote the taboo subject of homosexuality. That Kelly stressed manliness in his performances was not accidental.

In contrast to the emphasis on the formal integration of elements with the Freed Unit films, the Bob Hope, Bing Crosby, and Dorothy Lamour *Road* series of films reveled in disjunction. The series was popular and long lived, with the first film, *Road to Singapore*, released in 1940; four sequels followed immediately thereafter, with a fifth in 1952, and the final film, *The Road to Hong Kong*, was released in 1962. Produced by Paramount Pictures, the films capitalized on the comedic talents of its three stars and on Crosby's popularity as a crooner. These films stand out from other musicals of the time because they deliberately parodied other film genres and popular film tropes of the day, such as "Arabian nights"–style dramas and adventure films. The films also mocked the musical film genre of which they were a part; in *Road to Bali* (1952), Hope broke the fourth wall, advising audiences that they should go get popcorn during one of Crosby's musical numbers. Noncanonical musicals such as these—including singing cowboy films—which on the surface are merely silly and only sporadically discussed by scholars, can be very useful within the classroom precisely because they fall between the cracks of the standard definitions typically used for film musicals. The *Road* movies revel in being completely meaningless, even as they trace out a colonial history across the globe.[29]

THE 1950s

The 1950s brought television into its own as a form of entertainment. Bringing stars into the intimate space of people's living rooms triggered a larger shift in Hollywood films and in the viewing habits of audiences. Film studios embraced ways to expand the visual appeal of films through increasing their aspect ratio on the screen with widescreen technology and the use of 3-D. These technological changes brought a different kind of visual spectacle to films that television could not match. Along with television, a new genre of music—rock 'n' roll—became part of the mainstream. While in previous decades the music from film and stage musicals was popular music, rock music was a separate entity and overtook songs by Irving Berlin on the radio. A song from a musical, in other words, no longer equated with the notion of "popular" or youthful.[30]

The other major shift in film culture that shaped how musicals were made was the breakdown of the studio system.[31] The studio system had allowed "the majors" to dominate film production and distribution through long-term creative contracts and relationships with film distributors and exhibitors; it was the studio system that allowed the Freed Unit at MGM to flourish. While major studios such as MGM and Paramount continued to exist, they did so with considerably less industrial power. Although it might be difficult to see any difference between films made within the context of the studio system and those made after its disintegration, maintaining an awareness of the business practices of Hollywood when screening musicals is another way to engender historical thinking among students. The breakup of the studio system means that the history of the genre becomes even more fragmented than it was in previous decades. Blanket generalizations about studio styles become even harder to make. As a result, for the remainder of this section and chapter, discussion of individual films, rather than cohort of films, will predominate.

Even with the rising popularity of television, rock music, and a reconfiguration of teenagers as a separate category between children and adults, many film musicals of the 1950s could easily have been produced during the 1940s. Change in the movie industry rarely happens overnight, and with so many different cultural forces at play, it is not surprising that some studios followed a well-established path for producing musicals, while others experimented with new forms and new music. For the purposes of this section, the transition between the more traditionally styled and the more contemporary-styled musicals are represented by *Gigi* (1958) and *Jailhouse Rock* (1957).[32]

Directed by Vincente Minnelli and produced by MGM, with script, music, and lyrics by Broadway veterans Alan Jay Lerner and Frederick Lowe, *Gigi* is nearly overwhelming in its Technicolor visual excesses. As film critics pointed out at the time, the film bore a striking resemblance to Lerner and Lowe's Broadway musical *My Fair Lady*; both feature the transformation of the female protagonist into someone who is acceptable to society at large and, not incidentally, acceptable to the male protagonist who is fostering the transformation. Both are also set in the past, and in a foreign land, thus aligning them with European operetta-style musicals; the music is integrated within the narrative and is not marked explicitly as being a different mode of expression from dialogue. The music is standard Broadway-esque fare, with "Thank Heaven for Little Girls" as the most well-known song from the score. Other films produced during this era that are comparable in ethos to *Gigi* include *Singin' in the Rain* (1952), *Carmen Jones* (1954), *Funny Face* (1957), *Seven Brides for Seven Brothers* (1954), *Kismet* (1955), and *Summer Stock* (1950).[33]

In contrast to the above films, *Jailhouse Rock*, distributed by MGM and shot entirely in black and white, starred Elvis Presley as Vince, a young man imprisoned for manslaughter. While in prison, a fellow inmate takes Vince under his wing and helps to develop his musical abilities. After Vince's release from prison, he pursues a successful music career, although not without some serious trouble along the way. The songs for the film—including the titular hit "Jailhouse Rock"—were written by Mike Stoller and Jerry Leiber, coauthors of the twelve-bar blues/rock song "Hound Dog," among many other pop songs. In many ways, *Jailhouse Rock* is similar to all of the other backstage musicals produced before and since. While Vince might be more troubled than most characters of this subgenre—at least until *8 Mile*—the basic narrative trajectory is very familiar, and the construction of the stage (or any performance space) as a kind of utopia dates back to *The Jazz Singer*. The use of rock music, however, and the emphasis on violence as a nod toward realism and as a means to attract youthful audiences, is, however, quite different from earlier backstage musical films.[34] It is also a film that privileges the male voice and the male body, and the young male body in particular. While in some ways this focus is no different from the type of filmic attention paid to Gene Kelly and Fred Astaire, Presley's sexualized youth does set him apart from his predecessors, and it certainly distinguishes *Jailhouse Rock* from the majority of musicals produced during the 1950s. For a course examining constructions of gender, using *Jailhouse Rock* in conjunction with a variety of other musicals would provide ample material for class discussions.

THE 1960s

The late 1950s/early 1960s is typically marked as the long, slow decline of the popularity, and quality, of film musicals. During the 1960s far fewer musical films were being produced than in previous decades, and few if any of the films that were produced during this time made any attempt to rethink the genre conventions of the form.[35] The lack of quality is often attributed to the disappeared studio system and the rise of rock music. It may also have been that after more than forty years, audiences had tired of the types of stories musicals told and the ways in which they told them. Stars such as Fred Astaire and Gene Kelly, and directors such as Vincente Minnelli, were in the twilight of their careers in musicals, while newer generations of filmmakers and stars were interested in other modes of filmmaking. The 1960s through the 1980s saw new, independent producers and directors creating films that deliberately went against the kinds of large-scale, big-budget films that musicals had come to represent. The influx of European cinema—notably the French New Wave—prompted many American filmmakers to leave the soundstage and shoot on location, oftentimes using a handheld camera and an off-the-cuff style, not a methodology conducive to creating film musicals.[36]

Given that the narrative concerning the history of film musicals during this period focuses on decline, musicals typically associated with the decade are *Doctor Dolittle* (1967), *Chitty Chitty Bang Bang* (1968), and *Hello Dolly!* (1969). The first two films were primarily meant for children and received lukewarm reception by adult audiences. The last was an adaptation of the Broadway musical and starred Barbra Streisand, in what many critics felt was serious miscasting. All three films are generally considered to contain mediocre or unmemorable songs and strange casting choices, and are often characterized as boring. They are all perhaps best known for their inflated budgets and lack of box-office returns. In previous decades, the mediocrity of these three films would not necessarily make much of an impact on how the history of musicals is told. However, each film followed the other year by year. Given the relative downturn in the production of film musicals during the decade, these films have come to represent the state of the genre in the 1960s.

As in previous decades, many film musicals during the 1960s were adaptations of Broadway stage musicals. The key difference is that Broadway itself was undergoing a crisis during this period as well. Thus many of the musicals translated from stage to screen were shows that had been popular a decade or more earlier. This practice made movie musicals appear old-fashioned. That said, in the list of film adaptations of stage shows from this period, many of them are considered to be classic films, or, as in the case of *The Sound of Music* (1965), they are viewed as sentimental favorites. Adaptations included: *Bells Are Ringing* (1960), *Flower Drum Song* (1961), *West Side Story* (1961), *The Music Man* (1962), and *My Fair Lady* (1964). Perhaps the biggest difference between these adaptations and ones from previous decades is that none of them signaled a new aspect to the musical film as a genre and none of them attempted to integrate new film techniques.

As with every decade discussed in this chapter, the 1960s also saw a number of low-budget musicals; scholars rarely discuss them. However, this does not mean they are not worth using within the classroom. American International Pictures released a series of "beach musicals" featuring clean-cut teens Annette Funicello and Frankie Avalon singing bubblegum pop music. Musicals featuring Elvis Presley during the 1960s similarly did not reach for high artistic heights, for all of the strength of their star. These musicals targeted a clear demographic—screaming teenagers—and attempted to capitalize on stars and the fad of the moment.[37] Films along these lines also reveal the very complicated nature of the 1960s and the ways in which hippies, free love, drugs, and war protests could be erased by the dominant culture in favor of depictions of clean-cut and virginal teens.

The 1960s also saw the rise of the documentary concert film, with filmmakers such as D. A. Pennebaker following individual artists or bands, such as Bob Dylan in *Don't Look Back* (1967) or focusing on specific iconic concerts, as in 1968's *Monterey Pop*. Concert films are, in some ways, the quintessential "backstage musical," with an emphasis on how and why performances are created. And it is rather disingenuous to insist that such documentaries do not have plots; that the events depicted are true does not mean they are constructed as a narrative. While stretching the definition of "a musical" to include concert documentaries might seem to be too flexible, for the purposes of teaching, these documentaries can provide direct insights into the material, visual, political, and musical cultures of an era in ways that fictional films might not be able to do. Using musical documentaries also opens up discussions within the classroom regarding the definition of genres and the importance of framing topics clearly. A more pure definition of "musical" might preclude the use of *Woodstock* (1970), a film that has obvious uses for a course addressing the 1960s.[38]

THE 1970s

The historical narrative concerning the decline of the film musical that started in the 1960s remained unchanged through the early 2000s. In his essay "Of Tunes and Toons: The Movie Musical in the 1990s," Marc Miller notes that part of the reason for the decline of the movie musical during the 1990s can be traced back to the 1960s: "Usually costing $10 million to $20 million apiece when the average movie went for $4 million or less, most musicals of the late 1960s and early 1970s recouped less than half their budgets."[39] Not only were film musicals expensive, but also they often seemed out of step with modern filmmaking techniques and modern ideas.

However, while the 1970s is not discussed as a seminal decade in the history of the film musical, a number of significant musicals were produced during this time that tapped into changing audience expectations regarding film. Many musicals produced during the 1970s are now considered to be cult classics, and while some of them might not hit clear artistic heights, both stylistically and musically they nonetheless signify a clear break away from musicals such as *Hello Dolly!* or *Top Hat*.[40]

Another distinguishing feature of musicals in the 1970s was an emphasis on self-reflexivity.[41] Musicals, including *Cabaret* (1972), *Nashville* (1975), and *Lady Sings the Blues* (1972), played with traditional narrative structures, placed story and song in opposition to each other, and otherwise commented on the commonly understood discourse surrounding musicals as a whole. If musical films as a genre were understood to be utopian spaces filled with heterosexual romance and happy endings, many musicals of the 1970s reflected the Nixon-era disillusionment with the utopian promises of the 1960s. In *Cabaret*, none of the characters find a happy ending within the context of Nazi Germany, while *Nashville* and *Lady Sings the Blues* critique the music and performance business previously celebrated in movies such as *42nd Street*. Within the classroom, such a downward turn in musicals regarding an optimistic view of the United States is one way to open up discussions about why such optimism was fading.

Like *Nashville*, *Saturday Night Fever* (1977) is set in the present day, engages with contemporary issues, and fully acknowledges the ways in which the utopias imagined by musicals cannot be achieved. It also complicates the idea of the musical because none of its characters actually sing for themselves. Featuring disco music by the Bee Gees, *Saturday Night Fever* might be more properly classified as a dance film, and not a musical. However, even though the characters themselves do not sing the songs, the music nonetheless functions to reveal character motivations and emotions, and serve as a release from the forward momentum of the plot. Featuring John Travolta as a second-generation Italian American, the film was shot on location throughout New York City and emphasizes—sometimes quite brutally—generational, class, and gender conflicts. The link among *Jailhouse Rock*, *Saturday Night Fever*, and *8 Mile* is easy to trace, as are the connections between the Depression-era New York City as represented in films such as *42nd Street* and *Goldiggers of 1933* and the recession-era version of New York in *Saturday Night Fever*. Across the decades, musicals can be seen as working and reworking historically and socially relevant ideas.

Although a box-office flop in 1978, *The Wiz* is an important milestone in the history of musical films. As an all-black adaptation of *The Wizard of Oz*, it continues in the American popular culture tradition of the adaptation of white texts into African American contexts for primarily black audiences. The film also echoes many of the concerns of the 1970s, albeit through fantasy, by relocating the original location for the story's opening from Kansas to Harlem, New York, and by reimagining the heroine Dorothy as an inner-city schoolteacher.

THE 1980s

Perhaps as a reaction against the grittier, adult-oriented musicals of the 1970s, the 1980s saw the rise of the "teen musical," including *Footloose* (1984) and *Fame* (1980).[42] These are all films that for the most part feature recycled, rather than original, songs and that, like *Saturday Night Fever*, focus more on dance performances than on singing. The characters listen and react to music in ways that are similar to how audiences might, but in addition the music might also be nondiegetic. Unlike *Saturday Night Fever* however, these musicals have a fairy-tale orientation, with their female characters typically changed, and rescued by, the male protagonist. These musicals were also uniformly cast with white actors; the integrated cast of *Fame* is the exception. However, much of the music contained within these films originated with black singing artists and songwriters. Another very common aspect of the teen musicals was their extreme earnestness. There is no attempt to parody, comment, or reflect on the genre. Indeed, Jane Feuer sees much in common between the "teenpic" musicals of the 1980s and the musicals of the 1950s. Certainly their respective, conservative politic contexts are alike, which helps to explain those thematic similarities.

Television also had a significant impact on film musicals, or rather a particular channel did: MTV (Music Television) debuted on August 1, 1981. While the impact of a twenty-four-hour music channel, with its three-to-four-minute videos featuring rock, pop, and hip-hop performers was not immediately felt in Hollywood and its production of feature-length musical films, MTV fundamentally changed the popular landscape in terms of how music was experienced by audiences. No longer was it enough for a singer to be heard; he or she had to be seen, with music videos serving as commercials for both songs and performers.[43] But these videos also altered one of the basic premises of the film musical: that song and dance was in some way tied to narrative and character development. Music videos were an end unto themselves, and thus they made film musicals and their attempts to merge music and long-form narrative seem even more old-fashioned by comparison.[44]

Musicals that are typically ignored from the 1980s are hip-hop musicals; historian Kimberly Monteyne notes that nine musicals featuring hip-hop culture, music, and dance were released between 1983 and 1986.[45] Such musicals not only continued in the tradition of earlier all-black musicals produced by independent black studios but also reflected on more mainstream all-black musicals from Paramount and MGM, such as *Cabin in the Sky* and *Carmen Jones*. Monteyne draws a distinction between those hip-hop musicals created by those deeply invested in hip-hop culture and African American concerns of the 1980s, and those hip-hop musicals devised to capitalize on the trend of hip-hop music as it moved into the wider (white) mainstream. However, regardless of the level of authenticity, hip-hop musicals as a whole "deal with themes of urban space, race, youth culture, and performance," even as they address those issues in sometimes wildly divergent ways.[46] It is also important to note that hip-hop musicals, for all of their focus on blackness and the use of a musical style not typically heard in musical films, are still quite traditional in structure and plot. These musicals come from the same genre traditions as *The Jazz Singer* and *Gigi*, and should be considered alongside such films. For students who might be resistant to musical films, hip-hop musicals are an obvious point of entry; however, it is important to be mindful of the changes to hip-hop as a genre that have occurred from its earliest days until the present. Hip-hop manifested itself differently in the 1980s than during the 2010s, and these differences can be just as alienating (or amusing) to students as operetta.

While hip-hop musicals primarily targeted black youth, the 1980s also saw the resurgence of Disney animated musicals that started with *The Little Mermaid* in 1989; such films really hit their stride during the 1990s, but *The Little Mermaid* established many of the key tropes of this subgenre.[47] The songs were often composed by Broadway veterans—Broadway musicals were suffering their own economic decline during the 1970s and 1980s—and the narratives featured young protagonists in a coming-of-age tale variant, often rooted in classic, well-known myths and fairy tales.[48] As such, the Disney animated musicals can be characterized as carrying out the legacy of traditional Broadway musicals in ways that Broadway was no longer capable of doing.[49] By extension, these films could also be said to have carried on the legacy of the Hollywood musicals of the 1950s. Of course, such observations ignore the ways in which these musicals were also aggressively marketed by the Disney Corporation and how they fed into various other media, including toys, television spin-offs, Disney on Ice, reimaginings for the Broadway stage, and rides in Disneyland or Disneyworld. The film musicals were, in some regard, merely the vehicle for merchandising and propagating the Disney brand.[50] As teaching tools, while many Disney musicals might not directly relate to historical content, they certainly serve as examples of cultural, social, and economic histories.

THE 1990s

While not all of the film musicals of the 1990s were produced by Disney or animated, the decade nonetheless saw *Beauty and the Beast* (1991), *Aladdin* (1992), *The Lion King* (1994), *Pocahontas* (1995), *Hercules* (1997), *Mulan* (1998), and *Tarzan* (1999), just to list some of the key benchmarks. In addition to its extraordinarily popular animated musical films, Disney also released a series of live-action musicals that were, in general, less popular than their animated counterparts: *Newsies* (1992), *The Muppet Christmas Carol* (1992), and *Muppet Treasure Island* (1996), all of which, like the animated films, targeted young audiences, although not necessarily children.[51]

The Disney Corporation version of film musicals aside, few other American musicals during the 1990s generated much interest. Four exceptions were all released between 1994 and 1997, and all were, in some regard, prestige projects. The first of the four, *That's Entertainment! III* (1994), was released in celebration of MGM's seventieth anniversary and amounted to a large-screen "clip show" of cut or rediscovered song-and-dance numbers from well- and little-known films. As a teaching tool, the film certainly demonstrates stylistic and genre changes over time and can also be used to start discussions on how history can be "lost" and the reliability of archives. *That Thing You Do!* (1996) marked the all-American actor Tom Hanks's directorial debut. As a musical, it is a well-crafted, straightforward backstage musical about the rise and fall of a clean-cut 1960s pop group; it is only the film's place in Hanks's larger body of work that makes it of interest, although placed alongside *Hair* as an alternate view of the 1960s would result in interesting class discussions about that decade. The year 1996 saw the long-awaited film version of the famous Tim Rice–Andrew Lloyd Webber megamusical *Evita*. Starring the pop icon Madonna in the title role, the musical traces out a—heavily fictionalized—story of Eva Peron, the wife of Argentinian dictator Juan Peron. Primarily an allegory about star power more than it is a good history or biography, *Evita* generated a lot of interest in large part because of Madonna's presence in the film. Finally, 1997 saw the bio-musical *Selena*. This musical focused on the life and career of the popular Mexican American singer who was murdered at the age of twenty-three by a crazed fan. With the exception of *West Side Story*, there are few American-made film musicals featuring Latinx, and as such *Selena* is an important milestone.

But the decade that seemed to be dominated by Disney animated musicals also ended with what might be called the anti-Disney musical: *South Park: Bigger, Longer and Uncut* (1999). With twelve songs by Trey Parker and Marc Shaiman, the film explicitly mocks the Disney model of film musicals, but it is much more centrally concerned with issues of censorship, free speech, and the state of American politics. *South Park*, tied as it was to the long-running television program on Comedy Central and the unique style of its cocreators, Parker and Matt Stone, did not signify a major shift in the musical film genre. There were few, if any, musicals that precisely followed in its profane, R-rated footsteps. That said, the early 2000s witnessed a greater variety of film musicals than the 1990s, and while it is too early to say that the genre experienced a true resurgence, it did seem to have worked its way back into American popular culture.

THE EARLY 2000s

The early 2000s had a series of early milestones signaling that filmmakers had rediscovered the genre: *Moulin Rouge!* (2001), *Chicago* (2002), and *8 Mile* (2002) were all critical and commercial successes, with few similarities between them. *Moulin Rouge!* featured contemporary pop songs sung by its stars, was set in nineteenth-century France, and wove a Bollywood visual aesthetic throughout. *Chicago* adapted the cynical Broadway musical about crime and fame, using the songs as expressions of the characters' interior thoughts. It won the Academy Award for Best Picture. In contrast to the more obvious fantasies of *Moulin Rouge!* and *Chicago*, *8 Mile* was a semi-autobiographical, backstage hip-hop musical starring the Detroit-born white rapper Eminem as "Rabbit," a young man trying to launch his rap career in this black-dominated segment of the music industry.

If there was one identifiable trend during the early 2000s regarding film musicals, it was the trend begun by *Chicago*, that is, the adaptation of popular Broadway musicals into Hollywood versions of themselves, with *Chicago* serving as the gold standard for such adaptations. These adaptations were often framed as prestige projects, as a way of bringing more recent, but still classic, Broadway shows to a wider audience, including *Rent* (2005), *The Producers* (2005), *Dreamgirls* (2006), *Sweeney Todd* (2007), *Hairspray* (2007), *Les Miserables* (2012), and *Into the Woods* (2014). Produced by a variety of studios and by different directors, none of these films took similar approaches to their material.

The production of these musical films, however, did not mean that musicals would come to dominate the box office, that all musicals would be of high quality, or that audiences wanted to watch musicals in greater numbers. However, it was also the case that producers and audiences seemed willing to take some risks with the genre, and those risks were not just limited to the big screen.[52] Television shows such as *Buffy the Vampire Slayer* and *Scrubs* featured all-singing episodes, and the Disney Channel produced a string of made-for-television musicals starting with the blockbuster *High School Musical* in 2006. NBC began to air classic musicals adapted for television and broadcast as live events, to mixed reviews, starting with *The Sound of Music* (2013) starring country music star Carrie Underwood. While the popularity of such live events is questionable—whether audiences tuned in for the musical itself, or the possibility of a star failing during a live broadcast is an open question—it does highlight the sheer unpredictability of the "film" musical genre.

NOTES

1. There are of course musicals, such as *Chicago* (2002) and *Enchanted* (2007), that engage with and deconstruct the idea of singing and dancing as natural within the world of the film.

2. Daniel Chandler, "An Introduction to Genre Theory," Kubrick Site, August 11, 1997, http://visual-memory.co.uk/; Steve Neale, *Genre* (London: British Film Institute, 1980), 48.

3. Many scholars of stage musicals have explored the tensions between narrative and music inherent within musicals. See Scott McMillin, *The Musical as Drama* (Princeton, NJ: Princeton University Press, 2014).

4. These categories are taken from Rick Altman and Jane Feuer. For musicals grappling with issues of race—such as the all-black musical *Cabin in the Sky*, the idea that "the folk" are "natural singers" can take on very unfortunate overtones.

5. Rick Altman, *The American Film Musical* (Bloomington: Indiana University Press, 1987).

6. The musical *Grease* (1978) is an excellent example of how male and female characters in a musical resolve their differences.

7. For one take on the history of the genre, see chapter 5 in Jane Feuer, *The Hollywood Musical* (Bloomington: Indiana University Press, 1993).

8. Richard Barrios, *Dangerous Rhythm: Why Movie Musicals Matter* (New York: Oxford University Press, 2014), 3.

9. It should be noted that many African American films were explicitly designed to combat standardized Hollywood representations of African Americans.

10. The reason for this was mostly technological. Rather like the recent process of converting movie theaters from film to digital projectors, many movie theaters in 1927 were unequipped to handle a film that incorporated sound.

11. These films can also trace their roots further back to live performance genres.

12. Barry Keith Grant, *The Hollywood Film Musical* (Malden, MA: Wiley-Blackwell, 2012), 14–15.

13. The flip side of the "rural black life" musical was the "jazz club life" musical. Both types of films traded in very specific racial stereotypes.

14. As noted above, films produced by African Americans generally fell outside of the Hollywood studio system.

15. Jane Feuer, "Hollywood Musicals: Mass Art as Folk Art," *Jump Cut* (October 1980): 23–25.

16. Grant, *Hollywood Film Musical*, 15–16.

17. MacDonald also starred in a series of films with Maurice Chevalier in the early 1930s when she was with Paramount Pictures. However, she is chiefly remembered for her partnership with Eddy.

18. On stage, operettas are generally distinguished from operas by their light or humorous themes—it is rare for an operetta to be tragic—and light music. In addition, operas typically contain no spoken dialogue, and instead use recitative, while operettas do use dialogue. On film, an operetta is more often contrasted with musical comedies in terms of the setting and singing styles.

19. It is also the case that animated musicals might be more familiar to students than live-action musicals.

20. See Altman's chapter "The Folk Musical" in his *American Film Musical*.

21. For one of the few full-length studies of the singing cowboy films, see Peter Stanfield, *Horse Opera: The Strange History of the 1930s Singing Cowboy* (Urbana: University of Illinois Press, 2002).

22. Another strand of cheap "wartime musicals" was from Columbia Pictures, which produced a series of cheap films featuring Ann Miller before she left for MGM, and stand-alone "club performances" by jazz musicians Duke Ellington and Count Basie, who were looking to expand their audiences.

23. And of course there was *Yankee Doodle Dandy* (1942), a musical biography of songwriter George M. Cohan, which explicitly celebrated America and the American way of life but which does not directly reference the war.

24. Loosely based on the life of star Bill "Bojangles" Robinson, *Stormy Weather* does not completely ignore the war. It begins with Robinson returning home in 1918 at the close of World War I and pursuing a career in entertainment.

25. See the comprehensive book by Hugh Fordin, *M-G-M's Greatest Musicals: The Arthur Freed Unit* (New York: De Capo, 1975).

26. For example, between 1940 and 1946 "soundies"—short black-and-white musical films viewed on coin-operated, 16 mm rear-projection machines—were popular. These machines were typically located in nightclubs, diners, bars, and restaurants and featured self-contained musical numbers covering what seemed to be an infinite number of genres, from Hawaiian music to arias. Maurice Terenzio, Scott MacGillivray, and Ted Okuda, *The Soundies Distributing Corporation of America* (Jefferson, NC: McFarland, 1991).

27. Kelly's official screen debut was in director Berkeley's and producer Freed's musical *For Me and My Gal* (1942); he starred opposite Garland.

28. This is not to suggest that Astaire was never acrobatic, or that Kelly was not elegant.

29. A short-lived musical film genre during the 1940s was the "sports figure" musical, that is, the ice-skating musicals of Olympian Sonja Henie and the musicals featuring Olympian Esther Williams performing choreographed numbers in pools.

30. This is not to say that songs from musicals were suddenly dropped from the hit parade; the process took some time. However, rock music was a new genre of music—even with its roots in blues and gospel—that emphasized rhythm over lyrics in ways that marked it as completely separate from the types of songs featured in musicals.

31. The demise of the studio system was in part triggered by a series of antitrust cases decided by the Supreme Court in 1948. See Thomas Schatz, *Boom and Bust: American Cinema in the 1940s* (Berkeley: University of California Press, 1999), 324–28.

32. In terms of the style of music, precursors to *Jailhouse Rock* include *Rock around the Clock* and *Shake, Rattle and Rock*, both from 1956.

33. The last Hope/Crosby/Lamour collaboration also happened during this decade with *Road to Bali*.

34. Feuer notes that in the poststudio age, teenagers were one of the first audiences targeted by competing companies looking to maintain or spread their control of the market. Feuer, *Hollywood Musical*, 125.

35. Matthew Kennedy, *Roadshow! The Fall of Film Musicals in the 1960s* (New York: Oxford University Press, 2014), 208.

36. Although previous decades also had their share of independent producers or directors, the New Wave was a discernable movement in filmmaking that marked the wider changes brought about by the end of the studio system.

37. Certainly in earlier decades film studios capitalized on fads. As noted earlier, the backstage musical subgenre is the result of studio "bandwagon mentality." However, what is slightly different is that by the 1950s, studios—along with American society more generally—had come to recognize "teenager" as a category of consumer separate from children and adults. As a result, studios produced films that were meant for that new audience.

38. That said, concert films are not discussed within subsequent chapters. The focus is on more traditionally defined film musicals.

39. Marc Miller, "Of Tunes and Toons: The Movie Musical in the 1990s," in *Film Genre 2000: New Critical Essays*, ed. Wheeler W. Dixon (Albany: SUNY Press, 2000), 45.

40. To be clear, this is not to suggest that older-style films were not being produced; *Fiddler on the Roof* (1971) is a clear counterexample. Rather, the point is that the 1970s tends to be neglected in many histories of the film musical, and many musical films were clear attempts to rethink the genre, attempts that influenced musicals in subsequent decades.

41. As Feuer has noted, from their beginnings, musicals as a genre have historically had a tendency toward reflexivity. In part, this tendency is because musicals are often about celebrating entertainment itself. Jane Feuer, "The Self-Reflexive Musical and the Myth of Entertainment," in *Film Genre Reader II*, ed. Barry Keith Grant, 441–55 (Austin: University of Texas Press, 1995); Feuer, *Hollywood Musical*, 90, 126.

42. These two films were recently remade, with *Fame* in 2009 and *Footloose* in 2011.

43. Jake Austin, *TV-a-Go-Go: Rock on TV from American Bandstand to American Idol* (Chicago: Chicago Review Press, 2005), 200–202.

44. Music videos were not completely unknown prior to MTV; rather, it is the twenty-four-hour aspect of the channel and the sheer number of such videos that made the difference.

45. Kimberly Monteyne, *Hip Hop on Film: Performance Culture, Urban Space, and Genre Transformation* (Jackson: University Press of Mississippi, 2013), 39.

46. Ibid.

47. *The Little Mermaid* also marked the return of the musical film as the predominant format for Disney animated films; their films in the 1970s and 1980s had deemphasized music. "*The Little Mermaid*," in "Disney Theatrical Animated Features: The Complete Guide," ed. Paul Muljadi, *Wikipedia*, 2011, http://www.wikiwand.com/, 199.

48. Obviously there were exceptions; *The Lion King* (1994) is loosely based on *Hamlet*, and *The Emperor's New Groove* (2002) had an original story.

49. Regarding *The Little Mermaid* and the song "Part of Your World," *New York Times* critic Janet Maslin noted, "Any Broadway musical would be lucky to include a single number this good. *The Little Mermaid* has half a dozen of them." Indeed, Disney executives fostered the idea that Broadway had found a "spiritual home" in Disney animated films. Quoted in Miller, "Of Tunes and Toons," 47–48.

50. Ibid., 48.

51. Many of these films were released through Touchstone Pictures, a branch of the Disney Corporation.

52. Of course many musicals during this era, such as the musical biography of Cole Porter—*De-Lovely* (2004)—arguably took very few risks.

Chapter Two

Historical Concepts

How can students be helped to view the discipline of history as more than "just the facts" when, throughout their secondary educational experiences, the majority of them have been trained to take standardized tests emphasizing a fact-based model of historical thinking?[1] Dislodging the fact/content-based mind-set among undergraduate students is an ongoing process and a thread that will run through this chapter and its examples. Divided into three sections, this chapter uses individual films as case studies to demonstrate the means through which musical films can help teach students about different approaches to doing history. By emphasizing the "doing" of history and the ways in which the discipline constructs historical narratives, it becomes possible to move away from the maddeningly persistent idea that history as a discipline is concerned only with facts and that the facts speak for themselves.

Not all forms of historical methodologies are covered in this chapter. Instead, those methods most suited to student interests and career goals and those most relevant to the current state of the field are highlighted: public history, microhistory, and digital history. But before these specific methods are addressed, student learning must be effectively scaffolded. To use any of these modes—public history, microhistory, or digital history—of examining and writing about historical evidence, the very nature of historical evidence itself needs examination, as does the process of archival research. Thus, what follows first is a discussion of ways to use *Hair* as a means through which to foster student understanding of the differences between primary and secondary sources, before moving on to *Gigi* and the ways in which it can be used to prompt discussions about archival work. The remainder of the chapter is devoted to a discussion of *Singin' in the Rain* as a method of exploring digital history.

CLASSROOM DISCUSSION STARTERS

Each of the following sections invokes a different methodology, and questions to ask students are woven throughout each section. However, for ease of reference, those questions, as well as some prompts that did not fit within the narrative flow, are noted here. A question such as "how does this film help us to understand X," which might be usefully asked of each film, is noted just the once.

Primary versus Secondary Sources: *Hair*

- What are the differences between a primary and a secondary source? Is it ever the case that a secondary source might also be a primary source? If so, under what circumstances would that be the case?
- What are the differences between a scholarly and a nonscholarly source, and why do those differences matter? (Or what is the difference between a documentary film and a nondocumentary film?)
- What are the kinds of primary sources that might be used as evidence in a research project?
- How does this film help us to understand the differences between primary and secondary sources?
- What was the context (historical and cultural) in which this film was made?
- What argument is being made, and what assumptions underlie the argument?
- Why should we view primary sources with the same level of critical skepticism as secondary sources?

Archival Questions: *Gigi*

- What questions should be asked when dealing with primary material?
- When considering primary and secondary sources, how do we determine the reliability of the material?
- Within the discipline of history, what is a good process for developing a solid research question?
- In the song "I Remember It Well," which character is actually remembering the incident correctly? How do you know this?
- What might different versions of the same event reveal about that event?
- How might the history of a past event be written if the details of that event differ? Does it matter if those differences are small, or if those differences are substantial? (And how do you make that determination?)

Public History: *1776*

- What is public history? Can you list some examples? Is *1776* an example of public history? Is it a historical reenactment? Why or why not?
- You/your group has been selected to create a public history program for a historical event. In your planning, please consider the following: What aspects of that event would need to be left out? What kind of context would be needed so that that the audience would understand the historical importance of the event? Who is the target audience?
- Why might some aspects of history seem to be more "naturally" represented by some genres than by others?
- Is *1776* (or, more broadly, the film under consideration) "good" or "bad" history? What criteria should be used in making such a determination?
- Is "popular" or "public" history better, worse, or different from "traditional/scholarly" history? Provide examples of what you mean to justify your answer. (Another way to frame this type of question might be, Why do thousands of people go to visit historic sites and watch historical reenactments on the History Channel and yet very often say they hate history?)

Digital History: *Singin' in the Rain*

- What is digital history? Provide an example.
- Is—or should—"digital history" be considered as its own field, or is it really just "history"?
- In what ways does technology shape the ways in which we tell history?
- In what ways does technology shape the methodologies of historians?
- *Singin' in the Rain* spends a considerable amount of time on the "problem" of lip-syncing during a time of technological change. In what ways does this help us understand the impact of different technologies on the past?

Microhistory: *Idlewild*

- What is microhistory?
- In what ways do the sources we use shape the history that we write?
- Why might it be important to write histories about "average" men and women?
- Why is *Idlewild* so little discussed when considering OutKast and its contributions to popular culture? Put another way, why is it not part of the canonical history of film musicals?
- Is lack of popularity or failure one of the reasons particular histories become hidden from view, and if so who or what determines those "failures"?

- Is it possible for "average" people or "small histories" to eventually become part of mainstream history (something that is taught within a history survey course, for example)? What might trigger such a shift?

PRIMARY VERSUS SECONDARY SOURCES: *HAIR*

Year: 1979
Run time: 121 minutes
Rating: PG

There are key differences between primary and secondary sources. The preceding is an elementary statement, but it is not an easy concept for students to grasp. Even students who seem to understand that a primary source is something—to put it very simply—created and used during the time period being studied will often conflate the idea of "old" with "primary." For example, it is not unusual for students to perceive a painting from 1876 depicting the signing of the Declaration of Independence (1776) as a primary source regarding what the signing looked like. Of course, if one is interested in nineteenth-century attitudes about the signing of the Declaration, then this hypothetical 1876 painting could be used as a primary source in terms of nineteenth-century views concerning the eighteenth century, but such reasoning often confuses students. They tend to be wedded to the idea that an old source equates to a primary source, regardless of its context or content.

The other discussion to be had with students regarding sources is in terms of making distinctions between, for example, *American Studies Quarterly* and a blog post. In other words, it is important to acknowledge that within the category of "secondary sources" there are levels of trustworthiness and acceptability. A blog entry and an essay from *American Studies Quarterly* on hippies both qualify as secondary sources; nonetheless they are, of course, quite different types of secondary sources. While a blog post may or may not have been quite rigorously researched, it was not subject to the peer-review process and is generally not acceptable for use in a student research paper.[2]

An effective means through which to work through and discuss variations on primary and secondary sources is through the use of film; *Hair* is a particularly useful film in this regard. One reason for the film's efficacy as an example in terms of primary and secondary sources is that it has the "look" of a relic from the 1960s and is thus easily mistaken as an artifact from that time period. *Hair* and its music—in particular "Age of Aquarius" and "Let the Sun Shine In"—have become iconic representations of the 1960s. However, its looks and its music are misleading. *Hair* as a film is grounded in the ethos of the late 1970s and thus should be interpreted and understood as a secondary text about the 1960s rather than of the 1960s. As a primary source, *Hair* provides a way into the culture and history of the 1970s, although that point might initially be difficult for students to realize given how hard the film works to re-create its particular vision of the 1960s.[3]

One method of emphasizing the ways in which *Hair* as a film is a 1970s reproduction of the 1960s is to discuss the ways in which the plot of, and structure for, the movie version of *Hair* differs quite substantially from what was performed live on stage in 1968. As the cocreators for the stage version saw it, "Any resemblance between the 1979 film and the original . . . version, other than some of the songs, the names of the characters, and a common title, eludes us."[4] The stage musical was almost completely sung through with very little dialogue and impressionistic shifts from scene to scene and character to character. Relationships between people structure what little plot there is, with the Vietnam War constantly in the background.

In the stage musical, the two central male characters, Claude and Berger, represent two different responses to Vietnam, with Claude opting to enlist and Berger opting to burn his draft card. In the end, Claude is revealed to have died in Vietnam, and the iconic "Let the Sun Shine In" serves to honor his sacrifice. In the film, the characters operate in a similar fashion, up to a point. After enlisting, Claude sneaks out of the barracks for one last visit with his girlfriend, while Berger takes his place to keep Claude from getting into trouble. While Claude is away, his unit is unexpectedly shipped out and Berger is killed in action.

This moment of substitution of Berger for Claude is the clearest reflection of the difference between the two texts. The stage version of *Hair* was created and consumed during a tumultuous time in American history, but the outcome of the Vietnam War was not certain. Claude's decision to go to war is deemed an honorable, but incredibly sad, choice. In terms of the narrative, he functions as a bridge between "the silent majority" and "the vocal minority" in terms of opinions about the war. By the time the film version of *Hair* was made, the war in Vietnam had been over and lost for five years. American bewilderment over the lost war, and the position of the antiwar and hippie movements regarding that loss, resonate through the film in ways that could not have happened in 1968. The senseless nature of Berger's death, indeed the very ludicrous nature of the mistaken-identity plot device, underscores how the film is a 1970s reflection on the 1960s. Highlighting the differences between stage and film musical versions can be accomplished with a prefilm lecture about the stage version, asking students to focus on specific plot differences while watching the film, and then discussing why those differences might exist and what they mean.

Another way of highlighting the ways in which *Hair* is not a primary source when considering the 1960s is to place it in contrast to the classic 1969 documentary concert film *Woodstock*. Both films are loosely structured, have similar visual motifs, and address the same subjects: hippie lifestyle and culture, music, and Vietnam. But where *Woodstock* engages direct-

ly with and emerges from the ethos of the time period, *Hair* is a look back
and a particular interpretation of an era that had passed.[5] *Woodstock* is a very
long film; however, screening two short clips from each film and having
students perform a comparative scene analysis between *Woodstock*, a film
that captured a historical event, and *Hair*, a film created after a historical
event, allows for an active consideration of primary in relation to secondary
sources. Key questions for students to answer include the following: Who
authored each film? Who are the key people in each film? What was the
context in which each film was made? What is the argument being made by
each film?

It is doubtful that students will interpret *Hair* as nonfiction, and that might
impede the discussion in terms of differentiating between primary and secondary sources. Students often conflate a primary source with a factual one,
written/created by someone who experienced a particular historical event,
and that serves as evidence for "what really happened." If a source is fictional, they automatically assume it is a secondary source, albeit one that is less
than valid. However, it is important to keep students focused on the point that
a secondary source provides an analysis/reflection on, or a restatement of, a
primary source. Asking students to analyze the ways in which *Hair* analyzes
the hippie movement and 1960s attitudes toward the Vietnam War moves
them away from the fact that the film is fictional. Further, pairing the film
with a brief written excerpt of a 1970s examination of the Vietnam War and
comparing the textual secondary source with the filmic source drives home
the point that all sources must be carefully examined and that secondary
sources are interpretations of events from the vantage point of looking back
on the past.

ARCHIVAL QUESTIONS: *GIGI*

Year: 1958
Run time: 119 minutes
Rating: G

A standard assignment for a history course is to have students produce an
annotated bibliography prior to their writing the final research paper. Such an
assignment helps to scaffold student learning by having them think through
the research paper in advance of writing it. As part of an annotated bibliography, it is typical to have students write a two- or three-paragraph introduction
to the bibliography to frame the research project and the kinds of questions
that will be asked in the final essay. The problem, however, is that many
students are unused to conducting historical research. Thus, the issue of what
kinds of questions to ask in order to even embark on a research project can be
very difficult for them. Since history is about "facts" and "what really hap-

pened," the idea of historical research as a method of discovery and a way of asking questions regarding why and how something happened is a complex concept with which students must grapple.

An additional problem with historical research is that many students view textual materials as the only kind of sources available to them as researchers; such a limited view can also shape the types of research questions students elect to research. The idea of using alternate forms of archival material— music, photographs, or material objects—as part of the repertoire of primary material for a project is often a foreign one. The issue is one of competencies in research. Once students are conversant in the ways in which a source might be either primary or secondary, and the different types of secondary sources, they should also be exposed to the idea that historians can deal with "texts" in a way that is very broadly defined. The written word is hardly the only form of evidence available to scholars. In order to appeal to different learning styles, as well as different modes of doing history, students should be encouraged to think widely about potential research materials.

Gigi might seem like an odd choice to help students consider the archive and ways in which to engage in archival research. Film historian Rick Altman has illustrated that *Gigi* is in many ways the archetypical film musical in terms of how it structures its narrative.[6] In their turn, feminist film scholars have noted the inherently problematic gender constructs of a film privileging an older man's desire for a teenage girl.[7] Knowing about these more traditional interpretations of the film are important, because when using the film in terms of what it can teach about the archive, regardless of the intent within the classroom for the film, students will still react to its narrative structure and gender constructs first. One way to manage those initial reactions is to place the film within its broader critical and interpretative frameworks before shifting to more targeted discussions regarding research.

When using *Gigi* in class in terms of a mode of exploring research questions, it is not necessary to screen it in its entirety. Rather, one song in particular can be used to prompt discussion on the differences among memory, the past, and the historical record: "I Remember It Well." Performed by two of the oldest characters in the film, the song is a wistful recollection of their love affair that ended decades in the past, but it immediately becomes apparent that while both remember the feeling of having been in love, neither can recall the precise details of their relationship. The one categorically declares that they met at eight; the other just as forcibly asserts that no, it was nine o'clock and he arrived late. Throughout the song, neither of them can agree on a single detail.

After screening this particular number, ask students to come to a conclusion regarding which character is remembering the events of their past correctly. Almost invariably, students will claim that the woman correcting her former partner is in the right. The way in which the song is structured, with the male character asserting a fact first only to always be corrected, coupled with how costars Maurice Chevalier and Hermione Gingold perform it, easily leads to the conclusion that she is right, and he is wrong. However, neither character provides any evidence supporting their assertions of fact. What, then, might be considered good evidence? How might students go about obtaining that evidence if they wanted to prove that one character's historical claims were true while the other's was mistaken? These questions can then lead to a consideration of individual bias but, perhaps more importantly, a much wider concern regarding how to approach writing a historical essay. Both characters agree that the relationship happened and that it was, in some way, important to them both. They differ in the details, but are those details important? What else might be understood about that relationship if the details were concretely established? Or is it the case that the different versions of the same past event reveal even more about their relationship? In other words, how might the history of that relationship be written if the emphasis was on the whole, with the details glossed over or ignored? How might the history of that relationship be written if the emphasis is on the details and on the discrepancies between them?[8] All of these questions shape how one approaches an archive and how one structures a final research project.

"I Remember It Well" will not teach students how to physically dig into archival papers or how to perform a search in a library database. Rather, because the lyrics of the song are so clearly contradictory, what the song allows is for a consideration of how to ask good questions. Additionally, it can also reinforce the concept that when writing a scholarly essay, the author is engaging in a conversation with, and taking a position on, the primary and the secondary sources (which are themselves being placed in a conversation as well). The back and forth of the song, assertion and counterassertion, enacts the ways in which historians examine the same material differently and can sometimes come to different interpretations.

PUBLIC HISTORY: *1776*

Year: 1972
Run time: 142 minutes
Rating: PG

The National Council on Public History states that "public history describes the many and diverse ways in which history is put to work in the world. In this sense, it is history that is applied to real-world issues. . . . Public historians routinely engage in collaborative work, with community members, stakeholders, and professional colleagues, and some contend that collaboration is a fundamental and defining characteristic of what public historians do."[9] Examples of public history include museum exhibits, historical reenactments, and History Channel documentaries—the types of history, in other words, that target a more general, rather than a more academic, audience and that shares authority with a range of people in the process of knowledge creation.

Engaging with public history with the context of a survey course in history can be a difficult proposition. Survey courses tend to emphasize as much content as is possible within a semester. Students who will be teaching history at the K–12 level require survey courses to focus on content—names, dates, and facts—in order to pass subject-area teaching exams. With the semester time crunch, introducing the concept of public history would seem to be a waste of valuable class time within that context. However, there are multiple reasons for introducing public history as a methodology within the classroom. Within higher education, there has been a shift toward skill- and competency-based learning, with assessment outcomes targeting critical thinking and oral and written communication skills over memorization. Public history emphasizes good communication, collaboration, and application, all of which are competencies emphasized by organizations such as the Association of American Colleges and Universities (AAC&U).[10] Second, public history puts the focus on how historians function as knowledge creators and the ways in which they craft narratives to account for what happened in the past; public history is very much concerned with "the why" behind events. Finally, public history points to the many kinds of career paths open to a historian, an argument that has become more and more relevant in the age of declining history majors.

Many history faculty members, especially those who teach early American history, are quite familiar with the film *1776*. Unlike the Civil War, the American Revolution has not systematically infiltrated the popular culture of the United States.[11] Although Mel Gibson's *Patriot* (2000) focused on the Revolutionary War, and the HBO series on John Adams briefly entranced viewers, there is still a lack of popular culture material that resonates with Americans in the way that Ken Burns's documentary on the Civil War did.[12] The film *1776*, because it is both engaging and historically accurate, has often filled a void in the content gap when it comes to teaching early American history, but to reiterate, its content is not the primary focus here; *1776* works well within the context of teaching the fundamentals of public history. The film is rooted in the early days of the public history movement; demonstrates the value of collaborative work; and reveals how historians must construct historical narratives even when that narrative itself seems completely self-evident.

As with many of the films used as case studies in this book, *1776* originated as a stage musical, and it suffers a bit from a lingering "staginess," although that can be attributed to the time period and the formalities of the eighteenth century. The film *1776* tells a compressed history of the debates among the Founding Fathers surrounding the authoring, and then the signing, of the Declaration of Independence. The majority of the action takes place within Philadelphia's Independence Hall, which serves an emotional pressure cooker for John Adams, Thomas Jefferson, Benjamin Franklin, and others. In broad strokes, it is a story that every American knows: the Declaration of Independence was signed, America went to war with England, and freedom resulted. But because *1776* is a musical, that narrative is in some sense made strange. This strangeness can raise the issue of what the film's creators excluded in order to make room for the music, or the ways in which some songs engage with history—such as the love letters exchanged between John and Abigail Adams that is done in the style of a duet—and what that decision means for how we as an audience perceive the couple as historical figures.

The creator behind *1776*, Sherman Edwards, a former high school history teacher, spent ten years conducting the research and writing of the original musical. For the musical to work, however, he needed a collaborator, Peter Stone, who knew how to write for popular audiences and how to integrate the songs with the narrative. Both Stone and Edwards were committed to the idea of representing the Founding Fathers as human beings who were men first and icons of history second.[13] Their desire to have audiences emotionally connect to the Founding Fathers through narrative, while at the same time educating audiences that the decision to write, and then enact, the Declaration of Independence was very much a decision and not a historical inevitability, is exactly in line with the ethos of the public history movement as it emerged during the 1970s.[14] One thing to discuss with students, therefore, is why *1776* emerged at the time that it did and why audiences were so taken with the musical.

The process of creation, of matching songs to characters, revising or cutting scenes, telescoping certain plot points for dramatic effect, and ensuring that the story line is clear, is a very visible enactment of the process of writing a historical narrative within a collaborative, public history context. It is rare for just one person to write the entirety of a musical.[15] Typically someone writes the lyrics, another writes the music, and a third person is in charge of the story. This list of how a musical is written excludes the actors, set designers, and the rest of the behind-the-scenes crew who bring what is written to life. The lyricist must match words to a musical cadence, or a composer must create music that reflects the sentiment of a chorus, all with the end goal of pleasing an audience. The examples here are quite endless and are easily applicable to any film musical. But *1776* works particularly well as an example of public history because it reflects historical reenactments that often take place on the Fourth of July or in living history museums such as Colonial Williamsburg where trained docents (or enthusiastic amateurs) literally embody history. Additionally, as with Colonial Williamsburg and amateur reenactors, *1776* is very serious about its content and about getting the details as right as possible within a given framework.

An exercise using the film as a baseline to engage students in questions concerning public history involves having them collaborate in groups and creating a public history plan for a historical event. Questions for students should include the following: What would need to be left out? What kind of context would be needed so that the audience would understand the historical importance of the event? Who is the target audience? Why might some parts of history seem more "naturally" represented by some genres than by others? Students would be forced to make, and justify, choices that ensured historical accuracy, as well as narrative, and genre coherence. This type of exercise can also be easily adapted into an essay prompt, or even into a longer-term, local-history, service-learning project.

DIGITAL HISTORY: *SINGIN' IN THE RAIN*

Year: 1952
Run time: 103 minutes
Rating: G

Digital humanities (DH) is a relatively new discipline that has made uneven inroads within academia. Some institutions now hire tenure-track positions in the digital humanities, while others struggle to integrate technology in a meaningful and a productive way within the day-to-day teaching that occurs within the classroom. Almost as soon as this is published, this section will most likely be obsolete, because DH is moving quickly forward in an attempt to carve out a definition for the field and to find space on college campuses. However, for the purposes of this section, the working definition used here is from the "Digital Humanities Manifesto," which encapsulates many of the questions and tensions embedded within the field:

> Digital Humanities is not a unified field but an array of convergent practices that explore a universe in which: a) print is no longer the exclusive or the normative medium in which knowledge is produced and/or disseminated; instead, print finds itself absorbed into new, multimedia configurations; and b) digital tools, techniques, and media have altered the production and dissemination of knowledge in the arts, human and social sciences. . . . The first wave of digital humanities work was quantitative, mobilizing the search and retrieval powers of the database, automating corpus linguistics, stacking hypercards into critical arrays. The second wave is *qualitative, interpretive, experiential, emotive, generative* in character. It harnesses digital toolkits in the service of the Humanities' core methodological strengths: attention to complexity, medium specificity, historical context, analytical depth, critique and interpretation.[16]

As the above definition makes clear, DH focuses on new modes of production and dissemination of knowledge and has much in common with public history in its outward-looking, collaborative framework. The difference is in terms of the focus on technology and, to a certain extent, who the collaborators are. DH in academia very often fosters partnerships between computer programmers and humanities scholars, rather than between amateur and professional scholars as is often the case with public history. Another key difference between public history and digital humanities is that the former concentrated on exiting the dusty archive, while the latter in part arose as an answer to the question of how to effectively archive materials digitally, how to best use digital archive, and how to disseminate archival information digitally.

Although a recent revival of *Pippin* in London had its characters tweet, with the tweets projected onto the stage, as far as I know there are no film musicals confronting the digital age head on. However, the emphasis here is not on historical content but on ways of teaching approaches to history and on how to engage students with history as a discipline. Thus, a direct avatar is not necessary. Rather, the focus here is on using a classic film musical that confronts the impact of technology on a discipline and the kinds of questions technology can raise: *Singin' in the Rain*.

Singin' in the Rain begins at a major film opening, with the central character, Don Lockhart (Gene Kelly), answering a question posed by a reporter. Lockhart relates a version of his professional life, which, in voice-over, is often humorously at odds with the material shown about his life in the flashback. The question of the reliability of oral histories and officially reported histories is present from the start and is worth exploring with students. Lockhart's life story is a truncated version of the history of vaudeville and the impact that the advent of film—a new mode of producing and disseminating entertainment—had on it. According to *Singin' in the Rain*, silent film materially impacted those actors who could not adapt to the new technology. Soon enough, Lockhart is faced with yet another technological innovation: the syncing of sound with moving images.

Although much of *Singin' in the Rain* concerns the boy-meets-girl romance between Lockhart and Hollywood extra Kathy Seldon (Debbie Reynolds), it is important to keep students focused on how the film negotiates the history of "talkies" and the different reactions its characters have to the new technology. Some embrace it, others try to determine how to make money from it, and others—such as silent film star Lina Lamont (Jean Hagen)—are incapable of change. Lamont resorts to lip-syncing to Seldon's voice in an effort to hide her inability to shift from one mode of production to another.[17] While the parallels with DH are not exact, *Singin' in the Rain* can be used to engage students with fundamental questions about the role of technology in historical research, writing, and its dissemination. The film also works to open up questions about the ways in which history as a discipline has responded to the digitization of archives and the opening up of those archives to those who have not been trained in historical methods and thinking. Kathy Seldon's rise from talented amateur in the silent-film age to an early adopter and crucial trailblazer in the talkie era mirrors the different ways in which historians have grappled with DH.

Not only does the film raise the issue of the ethics of history, but also it can provoke students to think about how history is done and the relative stability of archival material once it becomes digitized. The scene where Lamont is forced to record, and rerecord, and rerecord a scene in her new talking picture demonstrates the fragility of new technologies, the scramble to make those technologies work, and the ways in which experts in a field must retool their expertise and become conversant in new ways of thinking about old material. Pairing the "Digital Humanities Manifesto" with this scene can assist in helping students make those connections and to form their own definition of the digital humanities.

MICROHISTORY: *IDLEWILD*

Year: 2006
Run time: 121 minutes
Rating: R

For the purposes of this section, a "microhistory" is informally defined as the variety of history that is traditionally disregarded by history survey courses at both the high school and college levels. More formally, microhistorians ask "large questions in small places."[18] In other words, microhistories use the in-depth research and writing of apparently small stories—often of little-known individuals, events, or places—in order to reveal larger cultural or historical issues. This branch of history was a specific reaction against large-scale, more sociological, studies in history. Proponents of microhistory, such as Carlo Ginzburg, claimed that a macro approach to the past served only to distort small-scale realities through overgeneralizations.[19] Rather than studying the "average man," studying the exception to the rule, or the "average exception," could bring historians closer to understanding the past.[20]

Although textbook writers and history faculty members attempt to include more than the standard grand narrative of US history, the fact remains that given the time constraints of a regular semester, it is often very difficult to push beyond the standard people (e.g., Thomas Jefferson and Franklin Roosevelt) and historical benchmarks (e.g., the Civil War and the Great Depression) that absolutely must be covered. These benchmarks reinforce the unfortunate tendency of historical narratives as represented in textbooks to segregate history by default, whereby African Americans, Asian Americans, and other minority groups are rendered invisible. For example, the standard narrative of the Great Depression rarely notes the devastating impact this economic disaster had on people and communities of color. The unfortunate side effect of such an approach is that the experience of white Americans is implicitly understood to be, and universalized as, the experience of all Americans.

The standard historical narrative also leads to another practice particularly prevalent among survey courses: minority groups are only ever explicitly included within history when an event directly relates both to the constitution of that group as a minority and to the larger, and more mainstream (i.e., white dominated), historical arc. The intermittent appearance of Native Americans prior to Reconstruction within US history textbooks, and their relative absence from those textbooks thereafter, is a case in point. For example, that Native Americans were actively engaged in and materially impacted by the US Civil War is rarely if ever discussed within standard history textbooks because the story of the Civil War is not "about" Native Americans.

Musical films can be used very effectively to engage students in discussions about how certain histories can become hidden, and the ways in which small, or even exceptional, stories through the use of microhistory can illuminate larger patterns. [21] *Idlewild* is a film explicitly concerned with African American history, and it opens up the possibility of discerning "hidden histories" by specifically engaging students with how focusing on small details can reveal wider patterns of importance.

Idlewild is also useful in thinking about different kinds of archives and of alternate sources that can help illuminate historical narratives typically excluded from a history survey course. Undergraduate students tend to conceive of primary sources as consisting almost exclusively of texts. Asked to name a primary source, students will almost invariably suggest something along the lines of "a diary entry." A song lyric, a musical notation, or a performative practice—such as tap-dancing—will not enter into their consideration when thinking about source materials. *Idlewild* pulls current African American performance practices together with images from the past, and this intermingling of different elements provides an entry into a discussion of how communities that have generally been written out of mainstream history preserve and perform their own histories. Further, the ways in which mainstream culture often appropriates these forms without understanding their wider significance or long histories can be examined; the genealogy of rap music is a case in point.

Set in the fictional town of Idlewild, Georgia, *Idlewild* takes place during the mid-1930s. An important fact to keep in mind when screening this film is that while it represents a particular era of American history, it does not depict actual historical events or figures. Another important aspect of the film is its anachronistic musical styles. While hints of swing and jazz can be heard within the songs written, composed, and primary performed by OutKast, the music itself is determinedly not of the 1930s. *Idlewild* is a hip-hop musical, and that genre of music often fits uneasily within the historical time frame established by the film. At least one film critic suggested that *Idlewild* was the hip-hop answer to *Moulin Rouge!* (2001), which had similarly juxtaposed contemporary pop music with an earlier twentieth-century time period. The built-in contradictions, however, open up the film to useful preliminary classroom discussions concerning how different eras are represented within popular culture, as well as the continuities that exist within African American performance traditions.

The plot of *Idlewild* is fairly straightforward. Two young men, Percival (André 3000) and Rooster (Big Boi)—the duo that comprises OutKast—are best friends and grow up into two very different lives. Dominated by his father (Ben Vereen), the introverted Percival helps out with his father's mortuary business while playing piano on the side at a speakeasy called Church, all the while dreaming of having something, anything, more in his life. In contrast, Rooster is a philandering husband and father to six children. He makes his money through bootlegging and trade with the criminal underground, but he is also the emcee at Church and runs the club behind the scenes; his troubles begin when those two sides of his life collide, and he must pay off his criminal debts using Church. Percival gets his chance at something more when St. Louis singer Angel Davenport (Paula Patton) comes to Church. It is later revealed that "Angel" stole her identity from an established St. Louis singer in her attempt to succeed as a singer herself. Percival writes a song for Angel, who makes her a star in the club; predictably, the two fall in love. Just as predictably, Rooster's bootlegging problems come to a head with a shootout in Church. The meek and mild Percival shoots Rooster's rival, thus saving his friend's life, but Angel has been killed in the crossfire. The film ends with Rooster reunited with his family, apparently having ended his philandering ways, and with Percival having picked up Angel's dreams of stardom to become famous on his own as a composer-musician.

Released in 2006, *Idlewild* was written and directed by the African American music-video director Bryan Barber. An all-black musical, it stars André 3000 and Big Boi, the hip-hop duo collectively known as OutKast. Critically acclaimed and wildly popular, OutKast was at the height of its fame when *Idlewild* was released, yet the film received very mixed reviews and is not particularly well known today. In terms of the history of film musicals, it falls outside of the normative history of genre. In terms of the history of the singing group OutKast, *Idlewild* is rarely part of that conversation either. It is considered a "minor" or "unimportant" film in ways that the subjects of microhistories often are. Discussion questions to consider regarding *Idlewild*, which will lead to broader discussions concerning the value of microhistory, include:

- Why is *Idlewild* so little discussed when considering OutKast and its contributions to popular culture?
- Is lack of popularity or failure one of the reasons particular histories become hidden from view, and if so who or what determines those "failures"?
- Can "small stories" add to our wider understandings about a particular time period?
- Is it possible for such small stories to eventually become part of mainstream history (that is, something that is taught within a history survey course, for example)? What might trigger such a shift?

Within the context of a US history survey course, *Idlewild* can fit within broader conversations concerning the ways in which histories are written and presented. As a result, it can be usefully paired with an essay such as John Hollitz's "The Truth about Textbooks," from his book *Thinking through the Past*, as another way to engage with the question of how certain histories are hidden or obscured, intentionally or otherwise.

Like many film musicals, *Idlewild* makes room for and excuses its musical numbers by using a performance venue—a nightclub—as well as people who make their living through performance. In that regard, even though the jobs held by the various characters are quite varied overall, the film nonetheless could be understood as perpetuating standard, stereotypical images of African Americans as "natural" performers. It is therefore important to confront those images and ideas head on and to explore how an "all black" musical such as *Idlewild*, one directed by an African American, simultaneously confronts and reinscribes popular culture representations of race in the United States that date back over a century. In other words, while an atypical musical film for its era, *Idlewild*, like a good microhistory, nonetheless uncovers important historical patterns and relationships.

Screening *Idlewild* when covering the 1930s and the Harlem Renaissance is also appropriate. Visually, and in terms of the overall plot, the film obviously engages with the 1930s, but it does so in ways that often run counter to the typical narratives involving African Americans during the period. As mentioned, the film is set in rural Georgia, and its lead female character, Angel, leaves her urban home for the country in order to become a star. Her geographic trajectory thus runs exactly counter to the standard narrative of the Harlem Renaissance and the Great Migration. In addition, the film as a whole examines a Southern black experience that refuses to acknowledge the presence of white Southerners. *Idlewild* thus determinedly celebrates rural, Southern blackness and, by implication, locates the roots of contemporary black culture within that experience.

CONCLUSION

As noted at the start of this chapter, *Idlewild*, *Singin' in the Rain*, *1776*, and *Hair* serve only as examples of the ways in which film musicals can be used to open up conversations about historical methods and the idea of doing history. Many other musicals could work in similar ways within the classroom. For a survey course that covers precontact through the Civil War, it might seem at first as though only *1776* is applicable, but it must be remembered that the issue here is not historical content but modes of thinking history. However, if putting *Hair* on the syllabus within the context of a survey course on early American history seems more trouble than it is worth, then perhaps use *Paint Your Wagon* (1969), which focuses on the California Gold Rush.

Using musicals films in order to teach historical thinking might be counterintuitive, but it can also be very effective. Indeed, the cognitive dissonance such a technique produces in students is a way to startle them out of old-fashioned, and history-resistant, ways of thinking. To teach historical content with a musical film has many obstacles, not the least of which is that historical figures did not sing and dance their way through the past. However, musical films can help students to understand the constructed nature of history; the different methods of writing historical narratives; and how historians approach their subjects, that is, differently than is traditionally assumed.

NOTES

1. One problem faced by history as a discipline is that the term "history" applies both to the discipline itself and to its object of study. It should also be noted that the culture wars of the 1980s and 1990s, and concerns over "revisionist history," played a crucial role in shaping Americans' definitions of history. The furor over the Smithsonian Institution's *Enola Gay* exhibit is an often-cited example of one of the battles in those culture wars.

2. Granted, with the slow shift toward open-access journals, this hardline distinction regarding the pedigree of online versus traditional print secondary sources is changing. However, students still need to be aware of the standards of practice for academic research and the ways in which sources can be assessed.

3. The film *1776*, which will be examined later in this chapter for the ways in which it engages with public history, could also be used as a way to parse out the differences between primary and secondary sources. I use *Hair* in part because it is such a chameleon in how it represents the 1960s.

4. Barbara Lee Horn, *The Age of* Hair: *Evolution and Impact of Broadway's First Rock Musical* (Westwood, CT: Greenwood, 1991), 118.

5. *Woodstock* is, of course, only one version of the events at the Woodstock concert. Like any other film, or historical account, *Woodstock* is an edited representation of the events.

6. Rick Altman, *The American Film Musical* (Bloomington: Indiana University Press, 1987), 21–27.

7. For example, see Valerie Walkerdine, *Daddy's Girl: Young Girls and Popular Culture* (Cambridge, MA: Harvard University Press, 1998); and of course Laura Mulvey's famous article where she theorized the male gaze: Laura Mulvey, "Visual Pleasure and Narrative Cinema," *Screen* 16, no. 3 (Autumn 1975): 6–18.

8. The film can also be used to discuss oral history and the importance of allowing subjects to speak for themselves.

9. National Council on Public History, "About the Field: How Do We Define Public History?" accessed October 14, 2016, http://ncph.org/.

10. In particular, see the essential learning outcomes as outlined in the Liberal Education and America's Promise (LEAP) initiative: Association of American Colleges and Universities, "Essential Learning Outcomes," accessed October 14, 2016, http://www.aacu.org/.

11. The relative success of the Fox network's *Sleepy Hollow*, which takes the story of Ichabod Crane and the Headless Horseman and transforms it into a story of a Revolutionary War solider transported by magic to the twenty-first century to fight evil, might signal a change.

12. One reason for the revolution's lack of a hold on the collective imagination of Americans is the lack of poignant images; the Civil War was thoroughly documented by photographers. Another reason is the ways in which the Civil War articulated issues of race in the United States and the fact that those issues are still debated in the United States. The revolution was, in many ways, much more abstracted.

13. Stuart Ostrow, *Present at the Creation, Leaping in the Dark, and Going Against the Grain* (New York: Applause Books, 2006), 43.

14. For a broad history of history as a discipline practiced in the United States, see Robert Townsend, *History's Babel: Scholarship, Professionalization, and the Historical Enterprise in the United States, 1880–1940* (Chicago: University of Chicago Press, 2013), 5. He briefly mentions the public history movement. For an overview of the development of public history, see John Tosh, ed., "History goes Public," in *Why History Matters* (New York: Palgrave Macmillan, 2008).

15. There are of course exceptions. Stephen Sondheim writes both the lyrics and music to his shows, although generally someone else writes the script. However, Meredith Wilson was completely responsible for *The Music Man*.

16. "The Digital Humanities Manifesto 2.0," Humanities Blast, accessed October 14, 2016, http://www.humanitiesblast.com/ (emphases in the original).

17. The situation is slightly more complicated than as represented here. Lamont has a terrible voice unsuited to talkies, while Seldon's voice (as the heroine) is quite lovely. That is, biologically, through no fault of her own, Lamont cannot make the transition, but the movie positions her as the villain and therefore responsible for her lack.

18. Charles Joyner, *Shared Traditions: Southern History and Folk Culture* (Urbana: University of Illinois Press, 1999), 1.

19. Carlo Ginzburg, "Microhistory: Two or Three Things That I Know about It," in *Threads and Traces*, trans. Anne C. Tedeschi and John Tedeschi, 193–214 (Berkeley: University of California Press, 2012).

20. Although there are many examples of microhistories, one of the best known is Natalie Zemon Davis's book *The Return of Martin Guerre* (Cambridge, MA: Harvard University Press, 1983).

21. Davis's classic microhistory *The Return of Martin Guerre* is very clear on this point.

APPROACHES

Chapter Three

Teaching US History with Musical Films

Starting with the English settlement of America and moving through the late twentieth century, what follows is a survey-history approach to the variety of film musicals that engage with particular events and people of US history. However, it must be admitted that the genre of musical films is to a certain extent limited in terms of the periods of US history the genre tends to cover. Musicals about precontact America do not exist, and no one has yet written a musical about the Teapot Dome Scandal of the 1920s. Nonetheless, even within a survey course, musical films can provide an excellent introduction to entrenched themes and ideologies within US history, especially when paired with a discussion about methodologies for studying history (see chapter 2).

Because room must be made within the musical films for songs, historical content and chronology is often pared down considerably. However, since musicals generally adhere to a strict formula, patterns about the ways in which history is represented can be traced. Whether used within a survey or a seminar course, musical films are therefore an excellent way to discuss the process of how history is written. For example, the notion of a generic formula as it applies to a musical can be applied to the familiar format used in history textbooks and help to unsettle student ideas that textbooks only contain unbiased facts.

One issue that may be of concern in using these films within the classroom is their length; certainly in a fifty-minute class taught three times per week, time management is a major concern, and the same holds true for a three-hour senior seminar held once per week. Films take up time, and it can be difficult to know if students are paying attention to what they see. There are a few ways around this problem. First, it is relatively simple, with a bit of contextualization, to screen excerpts of particularly relevant sections of a film. While a problem with such an approach is that students lose important context for the musical numbers, and it is sometimes harder for them to engage with the conventions of film musicals that structure song-and-dance numbers, it does leave more time for in-class work.

Another method is to use the "flipped classroom" approach to teaching. That is, students view the films—either online or through the library—before coming to class, and then clips of the film are shown as needed to help shape the discussion and in-class work. The disadvantage of such an approach is likely more than obvious to anyone who has taught before: students may elect not to view the films on their own. However, the same is true of trying to ensure that students do the readings before class, and there are many ways to counteract such behavior, pop quizzes among them. It is also effective to randomly select a student to summarize the films for the rest of the class; to include online discussion questions on the films as part of the course; or to require formal, but short, reflective essays on the movies. And of course if the films are dealt with seriously and substantially in the classroom on a regular basis, the majority of students will catch on to the fact that watching the film is as important as completing the assigned readings.[1]

CLASSROOM DISCUSSION STARTERS

As in previous chapters, some of these questions are broad and could be applicable to any number of films, historical events, or methodological issues. And as so often happens in the classroom, many of these questions can be asked throughout the semester to build intellectual and content-based connections from week to week. It is also important to note that questions raised in earlier chapters (e.g., What types of people are missing from this film, in terms of both race/ethnicity and sexual preference, and what types of professions are missing? Why might this be the case?) can and should be used in the context of a survey course.

- What similarities do you notice between the ways in a film musical is structured and the ways in which our textbook is structured? Why might that be the case?
- Compare and contrast the version of history depicted in [primary source document and/or textbook and/or scholarly article] with the version of history as depicted in [film musical]. What do these similarities and differences tell you about our understanding of the past? What do these similarities and differences tell you about the nature of historical writing?
- Why do you think that the musical left out [a historical figure, a particular event, etc.]? Would you have made the same choice, and why? What does

that tell you about the choices you might need to make for your research paper?

- Compare/contrast the ways in which [a particular group] is portrayed in the film with the discussion in the textbook/historical record.
- Why do you think a film musical was produced based on this historical event/time period, while this event/period has been overlooked? If you were to produce a film musical based on this overlooked event, how would you do it, and what would you include?
- In what ways does the music in this film provide an emotional connection to the event/character? Does this connection allow for greater historical understanding of the event/character, or do the emotions interfere with that understanding?
- What songs from [this time period] would you use if you wanted to create a historically accurate (relatively speaking) musical film about the period?
- The musical film ends at this point in American history. Knowing what comes next in terms of the history of the United States, and given the [gendered/racial/class] status of the film's characters, what might the sequel to this film be about? In other words, based on the history, what would happen next for these characters?
- "Meanwhile, in the rest of the United States . . ." This film has a very specific focus on [city/event]. Historically, what else was occurring in the United States at the same time as the events depicted in the film? How might you incorporate those events within the film?

AMERICAN ENCOUNTERS

The Disney animated musicals *Pocahontas* (1995) and its sequel *Pocahontas II: Journey to a New World* (1998) depict the histories of encounters between the Powhatan people of Virginia and English explorers/settlers. The first film emphasizes the relationship between Pocahontas and Captain John Smith, and highlights the well-known story of her saving him from execution by her father. The sequel addresses Pocahontas's journey to, and experiences in, London during the 1600s. Not surprisingly, both films spend considerable amounts of the narrative focusing on heterosexual romance, in the first, between Smith and Pocahontas, and in the second, between Pocahontas and John Rolfe.[2]

Also not surprisingly, both films take considerable liberties with the historical record; however, especially with the first film, these liberties can be used very fruitfully when placed in conversation with the writings of Captain John Smith. Over several decades Smith wrote of his encounters with the Powhatans, and there are many discrepancies between those accounts. Smith is well known to have been an inveterate self-promoter, and his relationship to the truth was flexible. Having students read short excerpts of his encounters with the Powhatans, such as his near execution, and comparing it to *Pocahontas* can promote discussions about how and why certain historical narratives are told and retold. And of course the entire nature of the reliability of primary sources is a crucial part of that discussion, with *Pocahontas* perhaps revealed as not so far removed from what historians know about the early English/Powhatan encounters as might be thought when first viewing the film.

Pocahontas and *Pocahontas II* are also valuable films because they represent twentieth-century ideas about the "noble savage" that can be usefully compared to ways in which Anglo-Americans have historically written about Native Americans. Thus, while chronologically the films fit easily with a week on British exploration and Jamestown, they are also films that can be revisited when discussing Andrew Jackson and Indian Removal.[3] The noble savage and the barbaric Indian are distorted mirror images of each other that prevent actual historical and cultural understandings of Native peoples; placing them in conversation can assist students in breaking down those dualisms in their own historical writing.

In teaching early American history, one of the problems is that textbooks tend to relate it not from a perspective of encounters, which allows for mutual agency—if not equal power—between Europeans and Native peoples, but from an implicitly European perspective, where it is "inevitable" that the Europeans will conquer. One reason for this bias is the relative lack of written source material from Native peoples;[4] another, is the typical authorial mode for tertiary sources: third-person objectivity. *Pocahontas* and *Pocahontas II* are both rather revolutionary in that they not only portray the relationships between the English and the Powhatans as a series of negotiated encounters but also do so from a female perspective. Further, the value of those perspectives is that inevitability of the English conquering the New World is undermined. While this undermining might seem to be highly romanticized, wishful thinking, and certainly it can be understood as such, it also reminds students that for the historical protagonists at the time, the final results of the initial encounters between Native Americans and Europeans was unclear.

COLONIAL HISTORY

This section will not repeat the ways in which *1776* can be used to teach the method of public history; rather, it will engage with the historical content of the film and how to use that content within the classroom. There are two key aspects to the historical content covered by *1776*. First, the reasons both for and against American independence are argued throughout the film using the writings from the Founding Fathers. Second, all of the colonies, both northern and southern, are implicated in slavery, and slavery is discussed as an economic system.

One of the running themes of this book is the need to unseat the idea among students that there is an inevitability to history, and *1776* does an excellent job in showing that the American decision to go to war with England for independence was not an easy one. Reading the debates in primary sources is one thing, but hearing those debates in songs such as "Sit Down John" highlights the emotional and the intellectual stakes for both Loyalists and Patriots. In terms of classroom activities and research projects, having students compare and contrast primary sources to the text and lyrics of *1776* is an obvious choice. Another, alternative assignment is to have students take those same debates and recast them in a different musical mode—punk rock or rap—as a way of rearticulating and translating the material.[5]

In terms of the early history of slavery, *1776*'s song "Molasses to Rum to Slaves," which bitterly articulates the Triangle Trade and the ways in which both the North and the South benefited from slavery, is crucial for several reasons. The song reminds students that slavery in the United States existed prior to the nineteenth century, and it existed through the thirteen colonies. The ways in which slavery as a system changed over time, much less the differences between geographic regions, are sometimes very difficult for students to fully grasp. The song starts that process of students understanding how deep the roots of slavery are in the United States and that those roots were part of an impersonal, economic system.

"Molasses to Rum to Slaves" explicitly discusses slavery as an impersonal, dehumanizing economic system, a point that is always difficult to get across to students. Slavery was an international system. The United States became the United States because slavery undergirded much of the necessary labor required to produce the raw materials the country needed for trade and production of goods. In the classroom, having students map out the economic relationships of slavery explicitly articulated in the song can serve as a starting point for other moments in the semester when those economic maps can be revisited and revised as, for example, how the international slave trade slowly ended while the internal slave trade within the United States flourished.

Because it is sung by a white man to a group of white men, "Molasses to Rum to Slaves" also highlights many of the ways in which the history of slavery and the Civil War in the United States has been represented. The Civil War is often represented as something that primarily impacted the lives of whites, and only secondarily as being about the lives of Africans in America. The song can lead to discussions about the lack of actors of color with speaking parts in *1776* as a whole, and it thus raises important questions about for whom the Declaration of Independence was meant. Looking at the film, the Declaration, and Prince Hall's (a freed black man) —1777 petition to the Massachusetts General Court requesting an end to slavery in Massachusetts helps to embed the point that African Americans were contributing to the American political system alongside the Founding Fathers.

1800s

Musical films about nineteenth-century America are relatively few and far between, although they are more abundant than those concerning the eighteenth.[6] While there are a few stage shows that address the Civil War, notably *Bloomer Girl* (1956), none of them have been adapted to film. In terms of teaching American history through musical film, if the suggestion here of *The Littlest Rebel* (1935) is deemed too problematic, there are certainly many other resources available on the Civil War that make up for any lack of musical films on the subject.

Films such as *The Littlest Rebel* are (in)famous for their pro-Southern representations of the Civil War, and when screened in the classroom they need to be carefully framed for students. Engaging with racist material does not imply that the instructor is endorsing racism; it is important to state this fact straight out and to keep repeating it. Students must be reminded that each film is a historical text with a particular point of view, especially in terms of the performance and representation of race.

The Littlest Rebel (1935), starring Shirley Temple, is likely not the first choice for a film about the Civil War, but as a musical, and as a view into how histories about slavery and the Civil War were rewritten by white Americans, it is very powerful. The effect of watching the very casual racism through Temple as the child protagonist can elicit strong reactions from students. Therefore, along with careful scaffolding, pairing the film with excerpts from Frederick Douglass's essay "Decoration Day" (1894),[7] in which he discusses how African Americans were being written out of American history, and which ties together the Civil War with Reconstruction, can assist students in discussing whether history really is written by the winners and the meanings of the Civil War.

One of the most effective aspects of *The Littlest Rebel* is its use of American folk songs as its musical palette. "Dixie" and "Polly Wolly Doodle" are among the featured songs. While not as heavily musicalized as other musical films, *The Littlest Rebel* nonetheless draws on nineteenth-century material as a means to authenticate its version of the Civil War. The folk songs from the film can be used in multiple ways within the classroom. Building a lecture on American nineteenth-century popular song, blackface minstrelsy, or the place of army bands during the Civil War is crucial in engaging with the Civil War and its aftermath as more than just a story about battles. *The Littlest Rebel* provides those opportunities.

Using *The Littlest Rebel* also allows for a group project where students, using songs from the period, can map out their own musical version of the Civil War. The complexity of such a group project can vary quite considerably, but a relatively streamlined version is to break students into groups within the classroom and have them outline their history of the Civil War. When would the musical start, and when would it end? What people, battles, and events would they include and exclude as scenes, and why? Finally, what songs from the Civil War era would they use to illustrate the plot points and the feelings of the historical figures involved? With some scaffolding, particularly in terms of American popular culture during the 1860s, asking students to create a synopsis of such a film musical in bullet point form can be completed in a single class session. The exercise encourages students to not just work collaboratively but also synthesize a wide range of material and think about the choices they are making. If the students in the class are particularly competitive, the exercise can be framed as a "pitch session" to the instructor-as-producer who will award funding to the best idea for the film after all the groups have reported out.

Outside of the Civil War, there are several musicals focusing on the nineteenth century that can be used in whole or in part, to cover certain topics, including *Paint Your Wagon* (1969), *The Shocking Miss Pilgrim* (1947), and *Annie Get Your Gun* (1950).[8] Set in 1848 and depicting the Californian Gold Rush, *Paint Your Wagon* stars Clint Eastwood, Lee Marvin, and Jean Seberg, none of whom are famous for their singing. In a gold rush boomtown suffering from a lack of women, a Mormon with two wives arrives, and his younger wife Elizabeth agrees to be sold off to one of the miners at an auction. After a series of plot complications, Elizabeth finds herself in love with two men—miners Ben and Pardner—and they agree to a regendered Mormon-like arrangement between the three of them. As the town grows, and the gold supply begins to diminish, pressures on the trio to become "civilized" increases. The town itself is eventually destroyed, and Ben decides to leave, allowing Pardner and Elizabeth to remain together as a more traditional couple. With a plot focusing on a ménage à trois, the musical is admittedly a bit odd. This strangeness, coupled with a run time of three hours, means that within an American history course, *Paint Your Wagon* does not need to be shown in its entirety unless the course focus is gender history.

Setting aside the complicated arguments concerning gender woven throughout the film, *Paint Your Wagon* provides a way of discussing western expansion and, of course, the gold rush. As the movie makes plain, miners in fact rarely made much money from mining for gold. Instead, the men who sold the pickaxes and other supplies became wealthy, but that did not stop thousands of men from making the journey.

However, since in most survey courses the California Gold Rush rarely takes up a significant amount of space in the curriculum, it is perhaps enough to screen the opening song "I'm on My Way" for students. This will provide them entry into the time period, open up discussion, and not take up too much time. The song, performed by an off-screen, all-male chorus, plays out over the opening credits filled with sketches of wagon trains moving across flatlands. The gendering here is important. The gold rush was dominated by primarily young men who wanted to get rich quick, an attitude expressed by the lyrics of the song. While the music for the song does not reflect nineteenth-century musical styles, its lyrics reflect ideas about the men who headed West to find their fortunes and serves well for a one-minute reflection/reaction essay about the place of the gold rush in American culture, especially as several of the stanzas are sung in languages other than English, indicative of the range of immigrants who also traveled westward.

The Shocking Miss Pilgrim can, like *Paint Your Wagon*, be used sparingly but effectively. *The Shocking Miss Pilgrim*, starring Betty Grable as Miss Pilgrim, is set in 1874. What "shocks" about Miss Pilgrim is her becoming a suffragette and advocating for equality in the workplace. One of the unusual aspects of the film is its focus on the ways in which technology—in this case, the typewriter—opened up opportunities for women to participate in the public sphere. This can be used to set up opportunities for later discussions regarding the impact of technology and inventions during the 1920s on the meaning of "women's work" and leisure. The early part of the film, when Miss Pilgrim first gains her degree in typewriting and is ready to face the workforce, provides solid commentary on the revolutionary idea of a woman going to work outside of the home. The musical number "Stand Up and Fight" takes place at a suffragette meeting and lays out the intersections between being taken seriously in the workforce and being taken seriously as a citizen.[9]

Unusually for a musical, the film does not end with Miss Pilgrim having to give up her career in order to get her man. It therefore opens up not only comparisons with *Annie Get Your Gun* (if used in the classroom) but also discussions about master narratives and the trap of the "inevitable ending." Within the emotional framework of the narrative, and the genre framework of film musicals, many students will feel as though *The Shocking Miss Pilgrim* does not have a proper kind of ending. That feeling of discomfort is important to explore.

Another important aspect of *The Shocking Miss Pilgrim* is its historical setting. While the focus of the film is on female suffrage, the events depicted would have been concurrent with the ongoing process of Reconstruction. The exclusion of Reconstruction can be made to serve as a reminder that the politics of women's suffrage existed alongside the politics of Reconstruction. The intersections between race and gender and how those intersections inflected the fractious coalition between the abolitionist and the early suffrage movements is an important social issue to address. *The Shocking Miss Pilgrim*, like many film musicals, provides that opportunity precisely because it is so silent on the question of race. Having students imagine the ways in which Miss Pilgrim might have been even more shocking, or by comparing Miss Pilgrim's (fictional) story to someone like Ida B. Wells, an African American woman who explicitly linked racial, gender, and social equality, helps to reframe the histories of both suffrage and Reconstruction.

An excellent bookend to *Paint Your Wagon*, and western expansion, is the heavily fictionalized musical biography of the nineteenth-century sharpshooter Annie Oakley: *Annie Get Your Gun* (1950). An adaptation of the 1946 Irving Berlin stage musical of the same name, the film can certainly be analyzed as a biography and, almost inevitably, in terms of its depictions of gender. But it is most fruitfully integrated within units on the end of western expansion, American popular culture, and the place of Native Americans in the latter half of the nineteenth century. Using the history of American entertainment—the musical's most famous song is "There's No Business Like Show Business"—*Annie Get Your Gun* portrays how the West was represented not too long after the frontier closed.

The plot of the musical follows the backwoods Annie (Betty Hutton) as she rises to the status of star in Buffalo Bill Cody's Wild West Show, all the while trying to win the heart of another sharpshooter in the show, Frank Butler (Howard Keel). Their romance proves to be difficult since she is a better shot than he is, and his male ego finds it very hard to take. In the end, Annie wins Frank's love by pretending to be a worse shot than he is.

What is most relevant about the musical for the classroom, however, is its depiction of the Wild West Show. The movie is quite clear that the day of western expansion and the "Wild West" are truly over, which is, in part, why Annie's facility with a gun is so threatening to Frank. There is nowhere for Frank to go in order to prove his masculinity; all that is left of the West are commercial representations of it. Paired with Frederick Jackson Turner's essay "The Significance of the Frontier in American History" (1893), the musical allows students to visualize what it symbolized to Americans when that frontier "closed." Placing the film and the text in conversation also illuminates the highly gendered and raced nature of the rhetoric of American exceptionalism itself.[10]

If used carefully, and if *Pocahontas* was screened earlier in the semester, *Annie Get Your Gun* also raises important questions about the place of Native Americans in the history of the United States. Cody famously hired the Lakota Sioux warrior Chief Sitting Bull in 1885 to be part of his "Cowboys versus Indians" set pieces, with Sitting Bull always endlessly defeated. In the musical Sitting Bull is portrayed by (Irish American) J. Carroll Naish, who adopts Annie into his tribe. Afterward, Annie sings "I'm an Indian Too," a number often cut from contemporary stage musical productions. In reality, Sitting Bull only managed to stay with the Wild West Show for a few months before tiring of performing a scripted version of himself and Native Americans for white Americans, a fact that the movie elides. However, the film is surprisingly frank about discussing Native peoples as now harmless and defeated, yet simultaneously as required to live under white surveillance. Having students research the tribes named by "I'm an Indian Too"—Seminole, Sioux, Navajo, Kickapoo, Chippewa, Iroquois, and Omaha—to find out how those tribes were impacted by western expansion and the Indian Removal Act can be a sobering lesson.

1900s–1910s

Finding musical films that engage in any way with the Progressive era is perhaps even more difficult a task than finding musicals about the Civil War. *The Shocking Miss Pilgrim*, while set in the 1870s and therefore just before when historians typically set the start of the Progressive era, can be used in that capacity. It analyzes not only women's suffrage but also the evil of "demon rum" and the need to control drinking, a top Progressive concern; it also has its own song-and-dance number. The white, urban, female base for the Progressive era, and the similarities between how women constructed themselves as responsible enough not to drink, and thus responsible enough to vote, is a connection that can be highlighted.

Films such as *Meet Me in St. Louis* (1944), set in 1904, or *Oklahoma!* (1955), set in 1906, while matching the historical time period, ignore Progressive politics completely. Films set in this time frame tend to emphasize nostalgic, small-town America and eschew explicit political concerns. Given the time frame of when these films were made, that is perhaps not surprising, but it is also the case that as a time period, the Progressive era is hard to effectively characterize from a filmmaking perspective.

One film that at least covers the overall historical time frame of the Progressive era, even if the specific politic issues are generally ignored, is the 1936 version of *Show Boat*, which begins in the 1880s and ends in the 1920s. Screening the 1936 version over the 1953 Technicolor version cannot be stressed enough. The earlier version adheres more closely to the 1927 stage musical from which it was adapted, and many of the Broadway actors who originated their roles on the stage were cast in the film.

On the surface *Show Boat* is a romantic melodrama with the history of American entertainment and music as its frame. However, since the history of American music is inextricably linked to the history of African

Americans, the film also grapples with miscegenation and what it means to be black in the post–Civil War era. One issue to note with students about the film is the way in which it is structured so that while the place of African Americans in Southern American life is highlighted in the earlier half of the film, as time moves on, African Americans are seen less and less. In textbooks, Reconstruction is often represented as "about" black Americans, while the 1910s–1930s are represented as "about" white Americans. Even the Great Migration cannot completely shake that construction. Through the structure of its narrative, *Show Boat* makes the construction of that textbook narrative more visible as African Americans are slowly erased from the movie.

As faculty members who teach American history survey courses know, covering World War I from the American perspective can be problematic. The Great War did not impact the United States in the devastating ways in which it impacted European nations, yet the nation greatly benefited from its aftermath. World War I provided the means through which the United States began its rise to world superpower. While the two films discussed here do not address that idea specifically, they do help to provide linkages from the Progressive era through the war to the 1920s and up through the Second World War.

Directed by Busby Berkeley and starring Judy Garland and Gene Kelly— in his first major film role—*For Me and My Gal* (1942) addresses the draft, draft evasion, and the dangers of wartime by focusing on the troubled romance between two vaudeville performers, Jo (Garland) and Harry (Kelly). On the verge of success on Broadway, Harry is called up to serve in the war, and so deliberately injures his hand to avoid service. In the meanwhile, Jo's brother is killed in the front. Understandably, Jo dumps Harry, and he attempts to redeem himself by volunteering to serve, only to learn that his hand injury is severe and permanent. Harry then goes to France to entertain the troops and ends up saving an ambulance convoy by destroying a German machine-gun nest. Of course, in the end, Harry and Jo are reunited.

A useful exercise to use with the film is to compare its visualization of World War I with actual images from, and primary texts about, the war. In stark contrast to the images and writing of the 1910s and 1920s, as a 1940s musical drama, and as propaganda for World War II, *For Me and My Gal* minimizes the brutalities of trench warfare. Comparing and contrasting those realities enable students to think critically about secondary sources. The film also exaggerates the role that America played during World War I, and in that regard it serves as another example of American exceptionalism and how Americans viewed themselves in relation to the rest of the world.

In contrast to *For Me and My Gal*, *The Great American Broadcast* (1941) focuses on the return of American soldiers from the Great War. However, it can also be understood as a film using the First World War to understand the

Second World War. While the musical does not touch the trauma of the trenches, the film is also useful in establishing a link to the 1920s, as the plot, which involves two returning World War I soldiers who pull together the first transcontinental radio broadcast, obviously makes it clear just how important radio was during this time period. The history of radio as related by *The Great American Broadcast* is completely false; however, the inaccuracies provides ample opportunity for students to conduct their own research into the history of radio in the United States and its impact on American culture. The presence of the African American dancing team, the Nicholas Brothers, also raises questions of the Great Migration, segregation, and the impact of World War I on the history of civil rights.

1920s–1930s

In contrast to the dearth of films about the Progressive era, the number of musicals addressing the boom/bust culture of the 1920s and the various economic fears of the Great Depression of the 1930s are, if not endless, certainly in good supply. Given the history of film within the United States, this is not surprising; the rise of film culture coincided with the decade of the 1920s.

Within a survey course, a key problem within the classroom can be unseating students' popular culture perceptions about the 1920s as an apolitical, fun-filled time. Reminding students that race, immigration, the place of women, the rise of consumer culture, and the international, political aftermath of World War I were also parts of the "Jazz Age" can be difficult. However, when used together, two films from the 1920s and one produced long afterward—*The Jazz Singer* (1927), *Hallelujah* (1929), and *Chicago* (2002)—can help to complicate students' understanding of the era.

With its long life on Broadway and regional theaters, and its Oscar awards once adapted into a film, *Chicago* is perhaps one of the best-known musicals in the United States. The film or stage musical could be a favorite for a handful of students in the class. Students who fall in that category might resist interpretations that run counter to their personal experience and enjoyment of the film. Allowing those students the opportunity to concretely articulate why they enjoy the film is very important. That said, there is no guarantee that students who have likely heard of the film will have seen it; it is over twelve years old, which might place it outside of the realm of popular culture for many students.

When discussing the film, it is important to have students acknowledge and unpack the ways in which it frames every event as a form of entertainment. This then leads to discussions about how *Chicago* fits within popular perceptions of life during the 1920s, as well as the rise of modern celebrity culture rooted within the decade. As a framing device for a unit on the 1920s, the film in its entirety is very effective because it both endorses and questions the idea of the "Jazz Age," embracing the stereotypical flapper image while highlighting the problematics of a mediatized culture. *The Jazz Singer* and *Hallelujah*, as products of the era, then further complicate the ways in which *Chicago* reconstructs the past, especially in terms of gender, race, and ethnicity.

Because *Chicago* structures its musical numbers as episodic fantasies playing out within the mind of Roxie Hart, it is relatively easy to screen portions of the film without too much loss of meaning. There are scores of texts by authors who lived through the 1920s that can be used in conjunction with *Chicago*. F. Scott Fitzgerald's 1931 essay "Echoes of the Jazz Age" is one of the more famous, and it works on a similar level as does the film in terms of being a reflection on what made the 1920s a unique decade, while also questioning and critiquing the memories of the era. At around four pages, Fitzgerald's essay is short enough to read in class alongside *Chicago* and provides links back to World War I and the Great Depression.

Entire books have been written about the place of *The Jazz Singer* in American culture, as well as what it articulates about American culture. For students, however, the film is very tough going because it is a hybrid film, part silent, part talkie, with the actors deploying silent film and vaudevillian acting techniques that to contemporary viewers appear very mannered and inauthentic. But there are also scenes that can still capture students' attention: the unscripted street scenes of New York, Al Jolson's calling out to a rambunctious audience that they "ain't heard nothing yet," his process of blacking up, and the depictions of Jewish religious ritual all provide teachable moments about immigrant life in urban centers, attitudes toward race, and another lens through which to view how and why the 1920s were christened the "Roaring Twenties."

Pairing scenes from *The Jazz Singer* with *Hallelujah* illustrates the differences between urban and rural, as well as between the European immigrant and the African American experience in the United States during the 1920s. Filmed largely on location in the American South, *Hallelujah* is a melodramatic, all-black musical about a sharecropper-turned-minister, Zeke. One question to ask students is why, in comparison to other musicals, so few framing devices exist for the singing and dancing that occurs throughout the film. The implications regarding the "natural" musicality of African Americans, and the historical racism, can then be articulated.

In watching the film, students will likely mistake the sharecroppers for slaves. African Americans are depicted as being completely unsophisticated, superstitious, family oriented, and devoid of any twentieth-century forms of technology. The initial focus of the musical on gospel and folk music will reinforce how students perceive the time frame for the film, even if the instructor is careful to situate it as about the 1920s. The representation of the time period is in stark contrast to the majority of musicals—and other forms of popular culture—about, or from, the 1920s. Even after the resident female troublemaker performs jazz music, the impression that the film is about the nineteenth, rather than the twentieth, century might persist. Unpacking this misperception, however, goes a very long way in helping students to understand the complex landscape of the United States in the 1920s. Not only are the differences between rural and urban, and between the lives of black and white Americans, brought to light, but also the relatively slow spread of technological and cultural changes is made apparent by the film. Asking students to research the number of households that owned radio sets and the geographic spread of radios—or other forms of technology—is one way of reiterating the disruptive idea that there was no such thing as a homogenous "1920s" for the country as a whole.

Having students compare and contrast the urban and the rural performances of *The Jazz Singer* to *Hallelujah* also brings out many stark nationwide cultural and economic differences in existence during 1920s America, differences that the Great Depression would only exacerbate. As the course moves into the Great Depression, ask students to map out the likely outcomes for the characters in *Hallelujah* and *The Jazz Singer*. Would Zeke and his family been impacted by drought or boll weevil, and thus formed part of the Great Migration? Might one of the children in the film been lynched? Would the inter-ethnic romance between Jolson's Jewish character and his Irish-Catholic girlfriend have survived? Such questions force students to look beyond the happy endings in both films to the historical realities their respective characters might have faced.

While musicals typically represent utopia, and certainly many musicals during the Great Depression followed that model, quite a number actively questioned the "American way of life," consumer capitalism, and the policies of Franklin D. Roosevelt.[11] The two films discussed for classroom use—*Gold Diggers of 1933* (1933) and *Ali Baba Goes to Town* (1937)—while not all inclusive of the economic turmoil faced by Americans during this period, nonetheless provide some very sharp commentaries. Both films were produced during the Great Depression and so can be treated as texts of their time, with all of the problems such sources entail. They were also produced at different points during the Great Depression and Roosevelt's efforts to counteract it and thus demonstrate how attitudes regarding the economic crisis changed over time.

Gold Diggers of 1933 is a canonical musical film featuring trademark phantasmagorical choreography by Busby Berkeley and songs by Harry Warren and Al Durbin. If there is no time in the semester to screen even portions of other films addressing World War I, "Remember My Forgotten Man," the number that closes the musical, will certainly serve. Inspired by the 1932 war veterans' Bonus Army march on Washington, D.C., the six-minute sequence shows the impact of World War I on the women who were left behind, and it re-creates World War I soldiers marching off to war, and marching back with injuries; their disillusionment when they returned home to bread and soup lines; and their final transformation into an army of homeless. The number actively questions American exceptionalism and notions of patriotism, and belies the idea that the end of the Depression will come easily.

If there is enough time, it is worth screening the entire movie that leads up to that final number. While the plot is a fairly standard "let's put on a show" backstage musical, it still clearly acknowledges the larger economic problems of the United States throughout. As chorines sing "We're in the Money" during a rehearsal, a group of men burst in and take away the sets and props because the producer is in debt to his creditors. A trio of chorines works together to find funding; of course they find it in the guise of a composer (and secret millionaire). In the end, the women find love with various wealthy men, and the show does indeed go on, with "Remember My Forgotten Man" effectively undercutting the traditional, happy, romantic ending of the movie itself.

Although the film ends with the impact of the Depression on men, the primary narrative arc of *Gold Diggers of 1933* focuses on the labor of women and how they negotiate both social and economic factors. It is useful to compare the images of these women and the impact of the Depression on them to the iconic photograph *Migrant Mother* (1936) taken by Dorothea Lange. Both the film and the photograph are very specific as to their depictions of women and the ways in which the Great Depression, an economic event that is often heavily masculinized, affected women. This can open up discussions regarding the types of labor that were acceptable for women during the 1920s and 1930s, and connections can be made back to *The Shocking Miss Pilgrim*.

For a more specific take on Roosevelt's presidency, *Ali Baba Goes to Town*, very loosely based on Mark Twain's *A Connecticut Yankee in King Arthur's Court*, is highly effective. *Ali Baba Goes to Town* features vaudeville and radio star Eddie Cantor as a hobo who inadvertently walks into a filming of the *Arabian Nights*, becomes a film extra, falls into a drug-induced sleep, and dreams that he is actually in Baghdad serving as advisor to the sultan. His advice to transform the country, filled with people starving in the streets and out of work, is directly lifted from Roosevelt's New Deal program; Cantor even mimicked Roosevelt's gestures and turns of phrase. The film actively critiques the New Deal policies—Cantor is not a particularly useful advisor—and it serves as an excellent means of staging a debate between students regarding the efficacy of New Deal policies.

1940s

World War II looms large in the popular American imagination, and as with the Roaring Twenties, it is well represented in films and musical films. There are both films from the period and those reflecting back on the time, but as with many of the films discussed throughout this chapter, the preference here is for films from the era. While not strictly accurate representations of either the front lines or the home front, musicals from the 1940s still capture attitudes, modes of speech, forms of dress, and landscapes of the period. Two films were selected as examples in order to provide some coverage of the European theater, Pacific theater, the home front, and issues of race and gender: *This Is the Army* (1943) and *South Pacific* (1958). They can be used in combination, used as stand-alone examples, used in full, or excerpted. [12]

This Is the Army, with music by Irving Berlin—including "Oh How I Hate to Get Up in the Morning"—connects the First World War to the Second. It begins in 1917 with the draft and follows actor Jerry Jones (George Murphy) to the trenches of France, where he is wounded. After armistice, the film flashes forward to 1941; Jerry's son Johnny (Ronald Reagan) has come of age. [13] The bombing of Pearl Harbor sets off a frenzy of enlistment, with Johnny refusing to marry his girlfriend Eileen because there is no guarantee that he will survive the war. The veterans of World War I decide to stage a fundraising show in support of the soldiers of World War II, Eileen joins the Red Cross, and Johnny and Eileen are married backstage before the men once again march off to war.

The film spends a considerable amount of time—about a quarter—on Jerry as he experiences boot camp and the trenches; it is certainly possible to split the film in half and screen the first part when covering World War I and a portion of the second half when teaching World War II. Although the initial fifteen minutes or so of the film set during World War II addresses the buildup to war and the impact of Pearl Harbor on the national mood, the bulk of the last half is primarily taken up with the stage show.

One of the more interesting aspects of the film is its shifting relationship between the idealization of war and army life as envisioned by Jerry in his World War I morale-boosting Broadway show and the actuality of wartime as he and his fellow soldiers experience it. While of course the trench warfare in *This Is the Army* is just as fictionalized as the rest of the elements in the movie, there is nonetheless an acknowledgment that what civilians believe war to be is nowhere near what war costs. Soldiers are hurt, and die, in the film, and their families grieve for them.

The film served as a fundraiser for the Army Emergency Relief Fund—a fact that is proclaimed as part of the opening credits for the film—and as a result can serve as a way of discussing the nature of wartime propaganda and the mobilization of the American people behind the war effort. While the second half of the film focuses on the stage show, it still provides ample opportunity for discussion about the cultural impact of the war. One of the first comic bits concerns a soldier who cannot kiss his wife because she joined the WACs (Women's Army Corps) and outranks him. The sequence lauds the women for showing their patriotism, demonstrates profound discomfort with women in the armed forces, and foreshadows Eileen's decision to join the Red Cross. While textbooks typically cover the rise of Rosie the Riveter in the home front, *This Is the Army* attacks the issue of gender during wartime in a way that might unseat student perceptions.

Another sequence in the film bears mentioning. About an hour and ten minutes into the film is the only point in which African Americans are acknowledged as forming a part of the war effort. The African American soldiers are allowed a full production segment and from one perspective are treated as equals to the rest of the men in the show. Certainly they demonstrate discipline, ability, and comic timing in ways that parallel the white soldier/singers. Students must be asked in what capacity African Americans were allowed to serve in the war. Why might it be important that these black soldiers performed as well as their white counterparts? Why were they featured in only one dance number, and what does that suggest about the broader historical context? Why were the troops segregated, and when were the armed forces desegregated? Students can also be asked why the black soldiers sing "That's What the Well Dressed Man in Harlem Will Wear" and connect the number to the Zoot Suit Riots in Los Angeles. [14]

Given the amount of material—from World War I through the beginnings of World War II, race, and gender—covered by *This Is the Army*, it is certainly feasible to use it as the only wartime musical in the course. However, *South Pacific* is a seminal film in many ways and can serve as a bridge to the civil rights movement of the 1950s. While it does not go into any of the gruesome details involved in the war in the Pacific, it does at least serve as a reminder that the European theater—the subject of so many popular culture representations—was a crucial part of the American war effort.

An adaptation of the Richard Rodgers and Oscar Hammerstein stage musical, *South Pacific* focuses on Arkansas nurse Nellie Forbush and her love for an ex-patriot Frenchman, Emile, who prior to the war, had been in a relationship with a local islander, the result of which was two mixed-race children. Much of the musical is concerned with resolving the romantic conflict between Nellie and Emile; she must overcome her disgust at discovering Emile's racial miscegenation. Along the way, the film also depicts life in an overseas army base, but that is not its chief concern, which is why it serves as an excellent transition between decades. Visually, the film is a bit strange. Director Josh Logan had the musical numbers shot using different color filters; for example, "Bali Ha'i" is suffused with green and purple, presumably to add an air of romance and mystery. It is also quite a long film, running just shy of three hours, and includes an intermission. Showing excerpts is probably the most effective mode of integrating the film within a unit on the war and using it as a transitional piece to the 1950s and the early civil rights movement.

"You've Got to Be Carefully Taught" is one of Rodgers and Hammerstein's most polemical songs. It takes place after Emile and Nellie have broken up; heartbroken Emile decides to join Lieutenant Joseph Cable on a dangerous mission to go behind Japanese lines and report on the movement of the enemy. The two men confront each other over their lost loves—Emile has lost Nellie because of her racism, and Cable cannot imagine bringing his local girlfriend home to his family—and then Cable angrily sings about how he was raised to perceive racial difference. One of the keys to this number is the absent Nellie; coincidence or not, the character is from Little Rock, Arkansas, site of the "Little Rock Nine," a group of nine African American school children who in 1957 integrated an all-white school under the watchful eye of the US National Guard. Although the events of the film take place in the middle of World War II, the film itself was released in 1958, creating an unintentional historical overlap. Having students investigate popular culture representations of African Americans during the 1940s and 1950s makes it clear that white Americans were "carefully taught" by social, more than familial, constructions about race and racial difference. This then connects to the material effects of such representations, as so clearly articulated in the song.

To create further connections, have students pay careful attention to the lyrics. Cable's song implicates the two-sided edge of racism. The victims include those who perpetuate racism as well as those who are the subject of racism, and thus the song in part echoes the words of Frederick Douglass in his autobiography. Helping students to see these historical connections using Cable and Emile's personal (but fictional) tragedies through the stylized reality of *South Pacific* forces students to confront racism as a social system and not just as a personal issue between two people.

1950s

While the 1940s in survey courses on American history can seem like a "single issue" lesson in content with near exclusive focus on the war, the 1950s widens out considerably in terms of topics and themes. The Cold War, teen culture, civil rights, and McCarthyism all vie for attention. The choice is always what to cut, what to include, and how to demonstrate the ways in which the Cold War, for example, intersected with civil rights. As noted in chapter 1, the 1950s saw the rise of rock 'n' roll music and the subsequent rise of film musicals attempting to incorporate rock within the genre; the generational conflict between musical styles often took the place of address-ing other forms of conflict.[15] As a result, while the previous and subsequent decades contain musicals directly addressing the concerns of their era, only one musical film from the 1950s addresses the more serious concerns of the decade directly. Surprisingly, that film is *Li'l Abner* (1959).

The plot for *Li'l Abner* hinges on the populace of a small town, Dogpatch, located somewhere in the South, persuading the federal government that their town is of value so that it is not used as a nuclear test site. Impending doom aside, most of the men and women in the town are more concerned about whether or not the Sadie Hawkins Race will occur.[16] The film is a satire, full of jibes about the South and American politics, and sometimes students have difficulty in reading the film as such. The actors play the situation absolutely straight, and students not paying close attention might not be in on the jokes. Visually, the film borders on the surrealistic, with highly saturated colors and sets that cannot be taken as anything resembling reality. However, the com-mentary expressed regarding nuclear weapons and America's place as a superpower work well in the classroom. The very fact that the town is slated for destruction by a nuclear bomb because it does not contribute to American capitalism opens up discussions regarding the military industrial complex and the ubiquity of the nuclear bomb in popular culture.

Because *Li'l Abner* is determinedly white,[17] it helps to underline, and then critique, the 1950s as a decade of conformist opinion. The filmmakers were resisting, and mocking, dominant political and social ideologies. This provides a way through which students can unpack some of their assump-tions about the decade and can function as a lens through which to read how the course textbook represents mainstream white Americans. *Li'l Abner* also prompts questions regarding the political usefulness of satire and can invite useful comparisons to contemporary news satire programs such as *The Daily Show*.

In terms of the civil rights movement, while no African Americans are featured within the film, the American Civil War and references to the Con-federacy are central to *Li'l Abner* and its satire. In the last two minutes of the film, Dogpatch becomes a national shrine when it is revealed that Abraham Lincoln honored the town's founder, Confederate General Jubilation T. Cornporn, for being such a terrible Southern leader that the North was able to win the war. Fundamentally, the film links the embedded contradictions between America's positioning itself as a moral world leader against the Soviet Union and the existence of legal segregation.

1960s

Hair is an obvious choice for a unit on the 1960s, but as it was previously discussed in chapter 2, other films will be used here. There are many documentaries about the 1960s, such as *Woodstock* (1970), that include focused music of the period, but this section maintains the overall theme of the book by discussing two narrative musicals: *Across the Universe* (2007) and *Hairspray* (2007), both of which are explicitly histories about the decade rather than films produced during the 1960s.

As noted in the first chapter, many musicals produced during the 1960s, including *Bye Bye Birdie* (1963) and *Beach Blanket Bingo* (1965), ignored controversial issues such as the civil rights movement. The films from this decade also constructed youth culture as completely apolitical, harmless, and disconnected from real-life concerns. It is worth screening segments of such films to compare them with protest footage from the era, or to ask students how the conservative viewpoints of these types of films implicitly pose arguments against feminism, civil rights, and the presumed leftist politicization of college campuses. Having students research both the college conservative group Young American for Freedom founded in 1960 and the origins of the 1962 Port Huron Statement, alongside a film representing youth culture such as *Bye Bye Birdie* or *Beach Blanket Bingo* with *Woodstock* as counterpoint can help illustrate the give and take of politics in the 1960s.

Mainstream Hollywood musicals from the 1960s were generally careful to avoid race as an explicit topic. In contrast, musicals about the 1960s produced decades later often incorporate racial concerns within the narrative. A relatively recent example of this practice is the musical *Hairspray* (2007). The first nonmusical iteration of the film was directed by John Waters in 1988, was adapted into a Broadway musical in 2002, and was then readapted as a musical film starring John Travolta in the pivotal drag role of heroine Tracy Turnblad's mother. Set in Baltimore in 1962, the film is a highly problematic representation of civil rights in America, but those problems make it extremely useful within the classroom setting. In a survey course, students will have already had the groundwork for the ways in which the civil rights movement had developed during the 1950s; this will prepare them for the movie. Before screening the film, either provide students with, or have them find, mainstream newspaper or magazine reviews of the musical. In class, students can then categorize the criticisms leveled at the film in terms of its racial, gender, and historical politics. *Hairspray* as a film defines the notion of "feel good," and it is important to prime students to look beyond its universal message of acceptance.

After screening the film, or portions of it, ask students to discuss whether or not, and why, they agree with mainstream criticisms of the film and what other criticisms they might make of it based on their knowledge of the civil rights movement. If students resist criticizing the film, have them discuss what themes and issues defined the early civil rights movement; reinforce that the movement was rooted in black churches and was concerned with the intersections between social and economic equality. Compare images of the process of desegregation as depicted in the film—with a young white girl as the leader of the movement to desegregate a local television dance show—to news footage from the era. Other issues to discuss include how the collective nature of the civil rights movement was in tension with ideals about American individualism, why the musical emphasized individual over collective action, and the reasons behind the parallel depiction in the film of racism as limited to a few white women rather than a systemic problem.

Hairspray is also a very useful film in (re)raising, and complicating, the issue of historical inevitability. The song "You Can't Stop the Beat" defines the rise of racial equality and integration in the United States to forces of nature. Desegregation is viewed in the film as a natural process. Implicitly, racial equality is defined as something that did not (or does not) need active work and participation in order to achieve. Highlighting this aspect of the film can lay the groundwork for the ways in which civil rights in America changed over the course of the 1960s and, if desired, can connect to contemporary rhetoric about the postracial society in America.

In contrast to the very specific concerns of *Hairspray*, *Across the Universe* (2007) is much broader in scope and more experimental in tone and structure, although it is still rooted in ideas about romance as it depicts the lives of its six main characters. Using the song catalog from the Beatles, with an emphasis on the Vietnam War, its characters explore various historical issues and moments that marked the 1960s, including the Detroit race riots, student protests and youth culture, and the drug culture. The film also highlights the centrality of music, and of the Beatles in particular, to the 1960s. The film begins in England, and for the sake of time, a large chunk of the movie can be skipped; beginning around thirty minutes in, while eliminating information about the characters, is quite workable.

Directed by Julie Taymor, *Across the Universe* is a film built around juxtapositions, coincidence, and impressions, a mode exemplified by the connection made between the death and funeral of a young African American resulting from the 1967 Detroit Riots and the funeral of a young white Vietnam War solider while the song "Let It Be" is passed along from character to character. It is important to establish the context for this scene, as the film itself does not provide any anchoring information. Rather, the movie works to establish an emotional resonance between the kinds of wars the United States was waging during the 1960s. Having students read Martin Luther King Jr.'s speech "It's Time to Break the Silence," where he connected systemic racism and economic disparity within the United States to the conflict in Vietnam, can help students to understand those moments.

Another effective scene in the film is when Max, a college dropout, is drafted and goes to the army recruitment center. With "I Want You So Bad" sung to ironic effect, Max's entry into the army is choreographed as a series of dehumanizing, mechanized moments on an assembly line as young men are swallowed by the military. The number, complete with the new soldiers carrying the Statue of Liberty through a Vietnam-esque landscape while they sing "she's so heavy," clearly questions an ideology of patriotic sacrifice. The sequence is very effective in making it clear why so many young men burned their draft cards. The film also raises the issue of college deferments from the draft and, by implication, the class difference that were part of the draft system.

1970s

While the opera *Nixon in China* (1987) offers some hope that eventually a film musical about the former president might be produced, as of this writing, none do. After the excitement of the 1960s, the 1970s is often referred to as "the stagnant decade"; the two films discussed in this section reflect that sense of malaise, albeit from quite different perspectives. The first, *Saturday Night Fever*, is an iconic movie, while the second, *Don't Play Us Cheap* (1973), is almost completely unknown. Both provide contemporary perspectives on the decade.[18]

It can be difficult for students to watch the entirety of *Saturday Night Fever*. The language is very intense, and degrading, toward the female characters, and there are two rape scenes in the latter half of the movie. While revealing of a reactionary attitude toward women's rights, screening the entire film is not necessary to convey that attitude, and the earlier half of *Saturday Night Fever* articulates its primary argument about life for young urban men in the 1970s.[19] Shot on location in New York City, the film also provides ample visual evidence for the state of American urban centers during the 1970s, and it touches on the racial and ethnic tensions that existed in the Northeast during the post–civil rights era.

Saturday Night Fever (1977) is a star vehicle for John Travolta as Tony Manero and in many ways functions as a character study. Without ever uttering the word "working class," the film makes it clear that Tony and his Italian American family are not economically well off, nor are they financially stable. As in many musicals, Tony uses music and dance as a mode of escape; the disco is his utopia. In screening the film, it is important for students to understand what Tony is trying to escape from and to have them engage in close scene analysis in order to understand the idea of stagnation as it runs throughout the film. While in the twenty-first century New York City has resurged as a financial and cultural center, safe for all ages, during the

1970s the city was in serious decline, something that is very apparent in the exterior shots of the city. If musicals have been used throughout the semester, comparing and contrasting the views of life in New York during the 1970s with life during the Great Depression can be one way of engaging with the cyclical nature of boom/bust economics.

Having students research the unemployment statistics for the United States during the 1970s, with particular attention to race and gender, is another way of examining the kind of life led by Tony in the film. Students can discuss where Tony, his family, and his friends fit within those statistics. Tony's father is an unemployed construction worker, Tony works at a hardware store, and his mother might need to enter the workforce to help keep the family afloat. Examining the economic data against the emotional reality of that data embodied in the film can then lead to a discussion about the changing—or static—nature of the American Dream and the cultural ramifications for white Americans during the 1970s who felt that dream might well be out of reach. Having this discussion in light of the dance competition sequence can be especially powerful for students.

During the last quarter of the film, Tony and his partner beat the competition in a disco contest. In the language of the genre, this win would typically cement Tony's position as the hero and as the consummate dancer; however, *Saturday Night Fever* undermines that trope. In a pivotal moment, Tony recognizes that he and his partner were not in fact the best dancers and should not have been awarded first place. The African American and Puerto Rican dancers on the floor were better; he won because of the color of his skin. This sequence raises issues of systemic racism within the small-scale and relatively low-stakes system of dance contests, but the argument can be extended to economic security, housing, and schooling, all issues of particular concern during the 1970s.

Set in an unnamed city is African American director Melvin Van Peeble's *Don't Play Us Cheap*, which he adapted from his stage musical of the same name. The musical embeds a fantasy element within its plot, but it nonetheless provides a window through which to view urban black culture and life during the 1970s, and it does so using the perspective of a black filmmaker. The plot is relatively simple: in Harlem, Miss Maybelle throws her niece Ernestine a birthday party. The party is crashed by two demons: Trinity and then Dave, both of whom are looking to cause trouble. Later, a bit of class conflict is introduced when the Johnson family arrives at the apartment with their son, who is attending college. A series of various misunderstandings, primarily romantic, ensue as a result of the demons' human impersonations, but in the end Trinity chooses to become human and stay with Ernestine, and Dave is literally crushed like a bug by Miss Maybelle after he transforms himself into a cockroach in an effort to escape the apartment.

The plot of the film actually does not take up much time; much of the focus is on the ebb and the flow of the party itself. Thus, many of the songs are not plot driven and spring more from various moments of the party as the spirit moves the guests to express themselves. As an atmospheric, insider's view of black urban life and the resilience of the black community, various group musical numbers can be shown. A brief moment in the last fifteen minutes of the film is where the political punch lies. Dave reminds Trinity that once he turns permanently human, he will be a "colored human" in America, deploying the n-word several times to drive home his point. It is a brutal moment in stark contrast with the rest of the film and likely will not have quite the same impact if shown completely detached from at least one other sequence from the film to serve as contrast. Asking the students why Peebles might have decided to disrupt what is otherwise a heartwarming and positive representation of black life is crucial, because it reframes the film as an artifact of the 1970s and the racial complexity of that decade, including school busing, Richard Nixon's election strategy, and the disproportionate number of African Americans sent to Vietnam. The eruption does not address any of these issues directly, nor does it directly address the longer history of Africans in America—arguably, as an all-black musical made by and for African Americans, there was no need to do so—but the shock value places students in the position of having to deal with that shock. Framing that moment first in terms of a creative choice and then broadening out to the specific historical contexts is a constructive method of allowing them to do so.

1980s–2000s

Most survey courses in American history are broken into two halves, precontact through the Civil War and Reconstructive through the early 2000s. It is also true that in the second half of a history survey course, the decades following the 1970s can be a gallop until the end of the semester. The 1980s onward are often skated over very quickly as the end of the semester looms and the present day gets within reach. The remainder of this chapter performs a similar move, with two films representing the 1980s and 1990s considered: *Wild Style* (1983) and *Rent* (2005).[20]

With the rise of Ronald Reagan to the presidency congruent with the rise of black street culture—hip-hop and rap—into mainstream white culture, screening a less-known hip-hop musical is pedagogically more important than screening a more well-known musical from the 1980s, such as *Footloose* (1984).[21] While less famous than *Breakin'* (1984) and its infamously titled sequel, *Breakin' 2: Electric Boogaloo* (1985), for classroom use, *Wild Style* is much more comprehensive in its depiction of hip-hop culture and the intersection between break dancing ("b-boying"), graffiti art, rapping, and MC'ing. *Wild Style* accomplishes this in part because it features a graffiti artist as the protagonist, rather than a dancer or a singer, as might be expected from a musical. This choice on the part of the filmmakers thus makes it an excellent choice for the classroom because it undermines students' expectations. *Beat Street* (1984), another early hip-hop musical, has similar strengths in terms of its attempt to engage with hip-hop holistically, albeit with a strong dose of Hollywoodization.

Wild Style makes it clear that hip-hop in its early years was as equally indebted to Latino culture as it was to African American culture, and this is an important point to get across to students, many of whom are not familiar with the early history of rap music. That said, some students might be more familiar with *Wild Style* than they know. As a seminal movie in the hip-hop genre, it has been sampled by other, more contemporary, hip-hop artists.[22] The first hip-hop feature film, it has appearances by many of the founders of the genre, including Grandmaster Flash, which mitigates the conventional boy-meets-girl romance.

It is important to help students see the connections between the domestic politics and rhetoric of the 1980s to the lifestyle depicted in *Wild Style*. While not an explicitly political film, it nonetheless directly represents ethnic minorities, urban decay, and poverty in ways that challenge the dominant discourse of the time. One way to allow students to see the disjunction between the film's rhetoric and the broader rhetoric of the decade is to compare and contrast its depictions of hip-hop culture with mainstream news media depictions of racial and ethnic minorities from the 1980s. Filmed in the South Bronx, *Wild Style* abounds with images of urban decay and destruction, but it also emphasizes those urban spaces and places that were highly meaningful to the citizens of the South Bronx.[23] Visually, the film highlights the tensions that existed in gentrified New York and the rising economic disparities between different parts of the city. Students can investigate the history of urban renewal policies during the late twentieth century and place those images within a larger national context and the national discourse about racial difference.

The movie's depiction of the South Bronx and New York City can also be usefully compared to musicals from the 1930s that address the Great Depression. This comparison can then lead to a structured debate concerning the efficacy of New Deal policies versus President Ronald Reagan's trickle-down theory of economics. Students should also be asked why films such as *Goldiggers* of 1933 and *Wild Style* represent poverty in the ways that they do and how the presence or absence of race in the films structures those representations.

Wild Style is hyperfocused on New York, and the South Bronx in particular. *Rent*, with its focus on the East Village of New York City, is no different in that regard. The action of *Rent* takes place over the course of one year, between 1989 and 1990, starting and ending with Christmas. Six of the original stars from the original 1996 Broadway production reprised their roles for the film, and the music is less "Broadway" in style and more toward the rock/pop end of the music spectrum. One of the first mainstream stage musicals with a narrative featuring young, gay and lesbian characters as sympathetic romantic couples, the show was very popular with college-aged and teen audiences, and that still generally holds true today.

There are three short sequences, running from two to five minutes each, that are the most useful in demonstrating the attitudes and concerns regarding AIDS during the late 1980s/early 1990s. The sequences, dispersed throughout *Rent*, primarily take place at an AIDS support group called Life Support. The first two sequences express the fears of the participants over their health, declining T-cell counts, and what it might mean when they become sick. The last sequence is a montage and focuses primarily on the breakup between two of the heterosexual characters—Roger and Mimi—interspersed with and placed in counterpoint to the slow decline and death of Angel, a transgender woman.

Rent has its roots in the tragic opera *La Boheme*; its depiction of dying and death is highly romanticized. It is therefore worth comparing this sympathetic vision of AIDS patients with contemporary media representations and to query those differences. It is also important to note a key similarity between the musical and news coverage of the disease: the diagnosis of AIDS equated to an automatic death sentence. In the twenty-first century, at least in Western countries, AIDS can be managed with medication in ways that were not yet possible in the twentieth.

CONCLUSION

One issue that instructors will face when using musical films as a means through which to teach students about aspects of American history is the focus that many of these films have on New York City. Many musical films are adaptations of stage musicals, and many stage musicals are set in New York. In part, this is the result of the need to justify characters breaking out into song and dance and the "backstage musical" trope. Broadway is, metaphorically at least, the home of musical theater. It is also the case that New York City is a financial center and a city that contains great ethnic and economic diversity; New York is a symbol, and musicals use it as such.

The New York–centric aspect of musicals can be mitigated by having a "Meanwhile, in . . ." assignment paired with such films.[24] For example, when screening *Rent*, have students investigate reactions to the AIDS crisis with prompts such as "Meanwhile, in San Francisco" or "Meanwhile, in the US

Congress." These investigations do not necessarily need to be done in depth; the question can serve as an excellent online discussion question, or as a small-group exercise with students generating compilations of concurrent reactions and events occurring elsewhere in the United States. The exercise requires students to observe patterns, to make connections, and to synthesize different events within a temporal framework. Over the course of the semester, "Meanwhile, in . . . ," if the exercise is deployed consistently, provides students with a self-generated study guide for midterm and final exams. Making the purpose of the exercise clear is therefore very important.

As noted in the introduction to this chapter, many significant events and people in American history are not addressed in film musicals. The coverage in terms of content is much less complete than with nonmusical films. However, as this chapter suggests, musicals make visible issues of race, gender, ethnicity, and class in ways that resonate across the history of the United States and that can open up discussions about those issues in productive ways, especially in terms of the intersectionality of those issues.

NOTES

1. No method is foolproof.

2. The relationship between Rolfe and Pocahontas is accurate in that the two did marry and have a child together, although the historical particulars of that relationship as depicted in the film very much depends on creative license.

3. It is also important to pay attention to the lyrics of the songs in *Pocahontas*. The song "Mine, Mine, Mine" explicitly refers to Cortes and Pizarro. This not only places English exploration within a wider European context but also is a reminder of the explicitly commercial reasons for European exploration and colonization. Paying attention to song lyrics is also an effective method of teaching students the skills of close readings.

4. Colin Calloway's *Dawnland Encounters: Indians and Europeans in Northern New England* goes some way in making it clear that Native peoples did, in fact, speak and write back to Europeans. Colin Calloway, ed., *Dawnland Encounters: Indians and Europeans in Northern New England* (Hanover, NH: University Press of New England, 1991).

5. The music genre selections here are not arbitrary. The stage musical biography of Andrew Jackson (*Bloody Bloody Andrew Jackson* [2010]) has a distinct punk music aesthetic, while Lin Manuel's *Hamilton* (2015) deployed hip-hop to great effect.

6. Other films, such as *Carousel* (1956), which focuses on small-town life in New England, and *Calamity Jane*, a film made in response to *Annie Get Your Gun*, would likely not add much to the curriculum. Musical films about Europe in the nineteenth century are much more prevalent, in large part because they are based on early twentieth-century American stage musicals. American stage musicals went through a period in which Europe as an exotic setting was very popular.

7. During the Reconstruction era, Douglass wrote extensively about national memory and Civil Rights; "Decoration Day" is just one example. It is available at the Library of Congress: Frederick Douglass, "Decoration Day: A Verbatim Report of the Address of Frederick Douglass at Franklin Square, Rochester, N.Y.," 1871, Frederick Douglass Papers, Speech, Article, and Book File, Library of Congress, http://www.loc.gov/. For background reading on Douglass and Reconstruction, see David W. Blight, "'For Something beyond the Battlefield': Frederick Douglass and the Struggle for the Memory of the Civil War," *Journal of American History* 75, no. 4 (March 1989): 1156–78.

8. Unfortunately, Disney's *Song of the South* (1946) is still not available. *Can't Help Singing* (1944) is another film dealing with the Gold Rush, although its main protagonist is a woman, and in that regard it is actually less historically accurate than *Paint Your Wagon*.

9. Jeanine Basinger, *A Woman's View: How Hollywood Spoke to Women, 1930–1960* (Middletown, CT: Wesleyan University Press, 1993), 15–17.

10. Since the film was produced in 1950, it also serves as a post–World War II commentary on the place of women within the United States. It can certainly be used very effectively in that way within the context of twentieth-century-history gender studies courses.

11. The 1944 film *Knickerbocker Holiday*, set during the 1640s, is a political allegory that sharply critiques the policies of FDR. Unfortunately, the film is not easily available.

12. The little-known *Up in Arms* (1944) starring Danny Kaye, is a very lighthearted view of the war in the Pacific and includes Kaye inadvertently capturing a Japanese platoon. Given its more serious tone and its engagement with race in American culture, *South Pacific* might connect more easily to other topics covered during the semester. However, depending on one's emphasis regarding World War II, the ways in which *Up in Arms* directly portrays America's war with Japan makes it a solid choice for the classroom. For more information regarding combat films as a genre, and the intersections between musical films and combat films, see Jeanine Basinger, *The World War II Combat Film: Anatomy of a Genre* (Middletown, CT: Wesleyan University Press, 2003).

13. The film also works as a long-term connection to the Reagan presidency and his use of media to sell his agenda.

14. If the focus of the course is on the home front, the film *Zoot Suit* (1981) is certainly worth screening. Adapted from the play of the same name, it deploys Brechtian techniques, mixing fantasy and reality together in ways meant to disrupt the narrative and distance audience members emotionally from the action so they can consider it intellectually. As such, it is a film that challenges conventional viewing techniques and genre boundaries.

15. There were of course films that sought to pretend that rock music did not exist.

16. For a course on gender, *Li'l Abner* contains a surfeit of material.

17. There is a solitary Native American character, although he has absolutely no place within the narrative. His brown skin seems only to serve more as point of visual difference to the rest of the characters.

18. *Car Wash* (1976) would also work well as a substitute for *Don't Play Us Cheap*.

19. For an in-depth analysis of the film, see Peter Steven, "*Saturday Night Fever*: Just Dancing," *Jump Cut* 23 (October 1980): 13–16, http://www.ejumpcut.org/.

20. Another potential film to consider regarding the length of the Cold War and the fact that the conflict between the United States and the USSR was decades long is *White Nights* (1985). Although more properly defined as a "dansical" than a musical, the connections it makes between international politics and national (American) racial politics can make it an interesting choice to screen in class.

21. Certainly *Footloose* could be used in the classroom to discuss issues of gender, as well as representations of the American middle class.

22. For example, see the Beastie Boys on their 2004 album *To the 5 Burroughs*. Justin Williams, *Rhymin' and Stealin': Musical Borrowing in Hip-Hop* (Ann Arbor: University of Michigan Press, 2014), 40.

23. Kimberly Monteyne, *Hip Hop on Film: Performance Culture, Urban Space, and Genre Transformation* (Jackson: University Press of Mississippi, 2013), 59–60.

24. This assignment takes its name from the popular Internet meme "meanwhile in . . ." For more information, see "Meanwhile In . . . ," Know Your Meme, accessed October 22, 2016, http://knowyourmeme.com/memes/meanwhile-in.

Chapter Four

Teaching Western Civilization with Musical Films

When teaching Western civilization using musicals, there are several issues to keep in mind. The first issue is similar to the one encountered when using musicals in teaching American history: a lack of coverage for certain historical periods, geographic regions, and types of people. The uneven ways in which available film musicals represent a larger world history can be an issue of concern. If film, and film musicals in particular, are to be used consistently throughout the semester for a survey course, one way to mitigate the lack of coverage is to intersperse nonmusical films throughout the syllabus. This method encourages visual literacy, continues conversations regarding adaptation and the value of sources, and can provide ample room for discussion regarding the different ways in which different film genres present history, and what that might mean for how historical events and people are understood.

Not only is there a lack of coverage in terms of the historical periods, but also there is a lack of coverage regarding women's history and the histories of people of color. Very frequently, when women and people of color are represented, those representations can be highly problematic, and even insulting, for students. The best way to deal with this problem is to directly confront it, and to do so constantly and consistently. Have students rewrite the parts for women in these films in ways that are reflective of current historical knowledge. Discuss the ways in which history textbooks may or may not do a better job in incorporating the histories of nonwhite people than many of the films. Simply asking students "who is missing?" when watching a crowd scene can help ensure that students will not simply sit back and watch even a segment of a film with unthinking acceptance. The concept of the "absent presence" is an important one and serves as a reminder of the ways in which historical knowledge is constructed not only through evidence but also through the interpretation of that evidence and by making decisions about who is important enough to include within the historical narrative.[1]

The second problem is an issue of language. Films that might be used within a Western civilization history course often feature languages other than English, which requires that students read subtitles, something that may cause a certain level of resistance to the film. Also, the musical language used in the film might be quite different from what students are accustomed to hearing. For example, the singing styles in Hindi-language films are particular to India and might inadvertently promote exoticization among students unfamiliar with Indian history and culture.

If an American-made musical is set in, or about, another country, the historical context in which the film was produced is especially important. If a Hindi-language musical might accidentally reinforce Orientalist attitudes among students because they are viewing it within their own culturally limited frame of reference, a mid-twentieth-century American-made musical will require a similar amount of contextualization. A film such as *Down Argentine Way* (1940), for example, needs to be understood within the larger political context of President Franklin Roosevelt's Good Neighbor Policy and the relationships between the United States and Latin American countries. While students might notice that a film deploys particular national, ethnic, or racial stereotypes, why those stereotypes are manifesting themselves within a certain film must be thoroughly unpacked.

But as with some aspects of the history of the United States, if musicals have been used fairly consistently during the semester, an excellent assignment is to have students map out their "ideal film musical"—complete with appropriate song choices about a particular period, person, or event. Such an exercise can also help facilitate discussions about why certain periods of history are better known than others and why popular culture tends to privilege certain types of histories over others.

Assuming that the relevant scaffolding for musical films has been addressed, there is still the issue that the scope of a Western history survey course is by its nature very broad. The periodization presented here may not align with how every instructor has elected to structure a semester that must cover over five hundred years of history across multiple continents. It follows a fairly traditional, quite broad, and Eurocentric method of periodization that should be adaptable for a variety of European history/Western civilization survey courses: ancient world (pre-476 CE), medieval era (476–1453), Renaissance and Reformation (ca. 1450–ca. 1650), Enlightenment (ca. 1650–ca. 1800), and 1900–present.

There are several reasons for using this fairly traditional form of periodization and for the emphasis on "Western civilization." Most industrialized nations have some form of the musical film genre, but the films are not readily available on DVD, or such films are not subtitled or dubbed. The global reach of Hollywood has meant that many international films remain highly localized; it is not economically feasible to distribute certain types of films to larger audiences. Given the ways in which film musicals are rhetorically defined as "American," musicals from many other countries remain untranslated and highly local. For example, incorporating the history of Japan within a world history/civilization course would be exceedingly difficult if film musicals are to be the primary teaching tool. The Japanese film industry has long produced musicals.[2] However, finding a Japanese musical that meets all of the following criteria can be an exercise in frustration: reflects the relevant era of history, is available, and is dubbed/subtitled with English. Also, certain countries at certain points in their histories are excluded from world history survey courses. "Mexico during the 1940s/1950s" is not a typical topic for a survey course, but Mexican ranchera and cabaretera films—with the former being pastoral romances and the latter best described as musical melodramas with film noir–ish undertones—were at their height during these decades. Ranchera and cabaretera films are highly revealing of Mexican society, culture, and history, but it can be difficult to fit such films within the limits of a broad survey course.[3]

However, for all of these problems and caveats of using film musicals to teach the history of Western civilization, one key benefit of doing so is the ways in which musicals highlight the nature of globalization and the ways in which the global becomes culturally specific. The use of musical films, by their very limitations, can reveal the Western- and Eurocentric master narrative of survey courses far more explicitly than a survey textbook. What areas of the world are excluded, when, and why? How might students create their own version of a world history course that is more inclusive or that has a different emphasis?

There is no perfect approach, and my using the more straightforward historiography in this chapter is an acknowledgment of the fact that many faculty members will be retrofitting the use of musical films within a course structure that already exists. For this reason, many of the in-class or out-of-class assignments discussed in terms of any one film in particular can, with some tweaking, also serve when teaching other historical periods with other musicals.

CLASSROOM DISCUSSION STARTERS

Many of the questions listed in the previous chapter regarding the history of the United States can, of course, be revised and used for a course about Western civilization. In addition, by formalizing the language somewhat, many of these questions would be suitable as short-answer or essay prompts as well.

- Based on the historical record, how accurate is the portrayal of the historical character(s) in this film? Are the discrepancies between the person's biography and the film's version of that biography important? Why or why not?
- Pay particular attention to the geographical features and set designs included in the film. Does the film represent the region and material culture of the era respectfully, or does it engage with particular American/popular-culture stereotypes? What, specifically, is "stereotypical" or "respectful"?
- How does language and aurality shape our understanding of a culture and of a country's history? For example, this film, while about [a country] uses the English language and Western musical styles, and is clearly meant for English-speaking audiences.
- Pay particular attention to the music used in the film. In what ways does music come to represent national characteristics, and why might that be important?
- Many of the characters—both real and imagined—are portrayed by actors who have no connection to the country/history being represented. Does this impact our understanding of the history of that country and its people, and if so, in what ways?
- Is it important to include the stories of relative unknowns within a historical narrative, or should the focus on "great men" be maintained? Why or why not, and how might the availability of evidence shape your answers to these questions?
- What are the differences between oral and written history, and what changes in process from speaking about the past to writing down the past? What does this tell us about the nature of historical evidence?
- In thinking about ancient societies and the histories of those societies, why might song be a particularly useful mode of remembering historical events? What does this tell us about the nature of historical evidence?
- In what ways does periodization obscure historical realities and limit our understanding of them? In what ways are such labels useful for cultivating an understanding of history? Where do you see the film screened today fitting within these questions of periodization?
- What is the role of popular culture in perpetuating certain kinds of historical knowledge or narratives?
- In what ways can the popular culture of a society be used to complicate historical understanding?
- How can fiction be used as historical evidence? Should fiction be used as evidence for historical events and people, and if so, what are some of the

dangers and benefits of doing so? What sort of contextual research must be done when novels or other words of fiction are used in practicing history? What can fiction teach historians about the craft of writing and narrative?

- When textbooks refer to "the people" in relation to historical events, what does that mean? To think about this question a bit differently, what are the benefits and dangers of generalizations in historical writing?
- Does the idea that some events or issues are too complex to set to music have merit when attempting to explain why musical films exist for some historical events and not others? Why or why not?
- Can art/popular culture—such as a musical film—be an effective political force for change? Why or why not, and if so, in what ways?

ANCIENT WORLD (PRE-476 CE)

Surprisingly, in 1955 MGM released a musical titled *Jupiter's Darling* starring Esther Williams set during the Punic Wars (218–201 BC). Williams portrays a Roman woman called Amytis, with musical film stalwart Howard Keel as Hannibal. While by no means a particularly historically accurate film in terms of its portrayal of actual events—the film is more concerned with the broad time frame—*Jupiter's Darling* nonetheless features many historical characters, including Fabius Maximus, Scipio Africanus, Mago Barca, and Maharbal.

The film begins with a historian, Horatio, telling a portion of the history of Rome. This framing technique opens up multiple avenues for discussing the nature of historical knowledge and narrative, especially in terms of the differences between written and oral histories, and ancient practices concerning the relating and preserving of historical knowledge. Comparing and contrasting Horatio's Fabius Maximus history with a few excerpts from Plutarch concerning Rome and Fabius Maximus establishes the nature of historical evidence as one of the overarching discussion points for the semester as a whole.

Since many of the real-life historical personages appear in the film only very briefly, one assignment is to have students research the biographies of these men, tracing out their roles in Roman or Carthaginian society and create a timeline of when and where they all would have intersected over the course of the war. While the character of Amytis is a complete fiction, she can serve as an entry point into a linked discussion regarding what is known about the role of women in Roman society and how those roles have been represented. By connecting the biographies of Roman men and women, a larger discussion regarding the kinds of evidence that survive from this time period, and how that evidence shapes our current knowledge of the past, can also occur. Finally, although it is an obvious point of discussion, examining what the film gets right and what it gets wrong about history and about its key historical figures is a useful mode of grounding the students' historical knowledge.

A key plot point for *Jupiter's Darling* involves Amytis assisting Hannibal by pointing out that his maps of Rome are inaccurate.[4] One way to capitalize on this scene is to have students map out Hannibal's actual progress toward Rome and to compare and contrast the different ways in which historians have mapped Ancient Rome. This scene can also serve as a jumping-off point for a lecture or discussion on the ways in which maps represent social and cultural constructions of reality and how they can serve as historical, as well as geographical, sources of information.

Another, and potentially more well-known, musical about the Romans is the adaption of Stephen Sondheim's *A Funny Thing Happened on the Way to the Forum* (1966). Inspired by the farces by Plautus (251–183 BC), the musical does not locate itself within a very specific historical time period beyond the fact that the events occur around two hundred years before the birth of Christ. However, depending on the nature of the course and the amount of time available, the film—or excerpts from it—does provide a way to discuss Roman literature, culture, art, and religion, especially if the film is paired with a few short excerpts from Plautus. The film also addresses issues of slavery, citizenship, and nation. As a broad comedy, these issues are played strictly for laughs, but because they are framed within the individualized experiences of characters for whom the audience/students cares, the film can help to ground discussions about the Roman Republic and its influence on world history. In addition, *A Funny Thing Happened on the Way to the Forum* frames its narrative from the perspective of a slave, which immediately raises questions concerning a philosophy of history. Is it important to include the stories of relative unknowns within a historical narrative, or should the focus on "great men" be maintained? And how does the availability of evidence shape potential answers to these questions?

MEDIEVAL ERA (476–1453)

While William Shakespeare and other playwrights wrote about Henry V and Richard III, the preponderance of musicals about the medieval period deal with the legendary figure King Arthur rather than actual historical figures. *The Sword in the Stone* (1963), *Camelot* (1967), *A Connecticut Yankee in King Arthur's Court* (1949), and *Monty Python and the Holy Grail* (1975) all, to a greater or lesser degree, engage with the legend.[5] It is also the case that film musicals historically located during the medieval period are almost invariably set in England and exclude any other country, although occasionally France will merit a (derogatory) mention.

There are multiple ways of handling this Anglocentrism. The first is to simply list the musicals that take place during the medieval era and ask students what, if anything, the films have in common. Exploring why the legend of King Arthur is viewed as appropriate for musicalization, while other medieval heroes and legends from other countries are not, is another area for discussion. The ontology of musicals as a whole, in which positive ideas about community are celebrated through the use of people singing in groups, can be used to highlight the relative stability of England as a cohesive nation-state in relation to other European countries. This focus on community can also help to explain why there are no musicals about medieval Italy or the fall of the Byzantine Empire. As mentioned in other sections of this book, having students create their "ideal musical" about a country other than England during the medieval period can serve as an excellent synthesizing exercise at the end of a historical period.[6] All such discussions and exercises raise important issues concerning periodization, historiography, and the nature of survey courses/textbooks, and engage students in concrete considerations about the nature of historical knowledge. And if this constant mention of the nature of historical knowledge seems repetitive, bear in mind that undergraduate students, and nonhistory majors in particular, tend to be quite wedded to the idea that history as a discipline is only concerned with facts and events "as they really happened." Intervening in such attitudes is constant—and yes, repetitive—work. Given the choices available for the medieval period, it is the farcical, and scattershot *Monty Python and the Holy Grail* that is the most appropriate for classroom uses. Although the film is the least musical, and the most profane, of the three listed, *Monty Python and the Holy Grail* engages in the least amount of romanticization when compared to the other musicals; its characters always seem to be covered in at least a layer of dirt, a stark contrast to other films. The film also has the advantage of being episodic in nature, and so screening segments of the film with very little setup in terms of the plot is easily accomplished. One potential problem in screening the film, however, is its strong language and critiques of religion and established social structures. *Monty Python* as a comedy troupe was committed to the idea of causing offense.

The film covers a broad array of topics, albeit in sketch comedy form: the differences between the lives of peasants and the lives of royalty; gender roles; the rules of primogenitor and inheritance; the place of religion in medieval life; the rivalries between France and England; and the general lack of cleanliness during the era. Depending on the time and the scope of course, screening a few clips from *Camelot* and *A Connecticut Yankee in King Arthur's Court* alongside *Monty Python and the Holy Grail* in order to compare and contrast changing ideas about the medieval period is a useful exercise.

The film's perspective on peasant labor, and the relationships between those who own property and those who do not, is likely the most generative aspect of the film for classroom use. Its anachronistic references to Marxist thinking provide a means through which later historical periods, benchmarks, and modes of thinking can be scaffolded for students. That is, students typically find the theories of Karl Marx to be hard going, but they will much more easily recall that King Arthur lost his temper at Dennis the peasant, who immediately responds to that display of temper with "now we see the violence inherent in the system." The centuries of economic and political repression against which Marx was reacting during the nineteenth century is not only explicitly enacted in this scene but also implicitly indicated in the relationship between King Arthur and his "trusty servant," the aptly named Patsy. Indeed, using the characters of Dennis and King Arthur as touchstones throughout the semester is one way to make historical changes both visible and more concrete to students. When addressing the medieval period, have students unpack why there is tension between Arthur and those whom he— nominally—rules and how that relates to the feudal system. As the semester continues, return to the pair to examine the ways in which those feudal and class tensions manifested themselves as the economic and social systems changed.

The scene between Arthur and the peasants is also useful in terms of revealing the very different ways in which contemporary people conceptualize ideas of nationality and nation. Toward the beginning of the exchange with Arthur, the female peasant bluntly asks her king, "Who are the Britons?" While within the context of the scene, this question could be viewed as her offering another challenge to Arthur's authority, it also signifies a very real medieval worldview. Within medieval Europe, life was highly localized, and the "imagined community" of a larger, cohesive nation and people connected by a single idea of that nation did not exist. Another way to approach the film, then, is through the Arthurian legends and the notion of "nation" that is being built through stories of one great king who can gather together men for a single purpose.

As indicated by the title, the other overarching theme of *Monty Python and the Holy Grail* is the Christian religion. The film of course takes a very tongue-in-cheek view of religion and of its role in society, and yet it does also reference the medieval sensibility in terms of the belief that God directly shaped people and actions. In the animated sequence in which God sets the knights on the quest for the Holy Grail, animator Terry Gilliam borrowed heavily from medieval paintings and illuminated manuscripts for his imagery.[7] Visually, the scene is thus very reflective of medieval concepts of God and can be used as part of a lecture on the visual culture of the medieval period by having students engage in a comparative visual analysis of both sets of material.

While the visual references often make direct nods to medieval culture, the behavior of God in the scene, and his admonition that the knights stop groveling, is anachronistic. A medieval God expected groveling, but a God of the 1970s would not have done so. Therefore, one way to address this scene is to break the class into groups, with half arguing the ways in which the scene is true to the period, and half arguing the ways in which the scene is closer to modern conceptions of God. The next step is for students to explain the historical reasons behind why such a transformation took place regarding concepts of God, explanations that must refer to the Reformation and the rise of Protestants.

RENAISSANCE AND REFORMATION (CA. 1450–CA. 1650)

The *Vagabond King* (1956) is an adaptation of the 1925 operetta by Rudolf Friml and as such features musical and acting styles that will likely provoke laughter—or groans—from students.[8] As might be expected of a 1950s Hollywood musical based on a 1920s text, the film tells a highly fictionalized account of how, in 1461, the fifteenth-century poet, and thief, Francois Villon became "king for a day" of France and defended Paris against the invading forces of the Duke of Burgundy. While Villon was never "king for a day," he was both a famous poet and famous criminal, and the Duke of Burgundy—Charles I ("The Bold")—was indeed attempting to wrest power away from King Louis XI.

The political and military struggle between Louis XI and Charles I forms a backdrop to the romantic difficulties of Villon, but the film can nonetheless be used to highlight ongoing tensions that existed in Europe regarding the evolution of the modern nation-state. The film also hints at many of the underlying problems within France that would eventually lead to the French Revolution and thus can also serve as a precursor to that era of history and to the use in the classroom of the musical *Les Miserables* (2012).

The Vagabond King is also a means of introducing some of Villon's poetry into the class as a primary source of information regarding the courtly ideal and the actual lives of the lowly.[9] The film can also function to engage students with the concept of "history from below"; while by no means a peasant, Villon was certainly not royalty, nor did he live his life among the elite. His biography, and the ways in which the film elects to portray it, raises important questions about romanticizing the lower classes, and the types of evidence available to historians when studying periods of time or groups of people when illiteracy was the norm, rather than the exception. Further, asking students how reliable Villon is as a source in light of his criminal history makes it plain the ways in which textual sources cannot be taken at face value.

The film does not delve into much detail regarding the history behind the conflict between Louis XI and Charles I. Indeed, the king is initially characterized as a vain despot who is constantly mocked—in verse—by Villon. The historical inaccuracy can be used most obviously by having students research or discuss where the film gets it wrong, and right, about both men. This can then lead to a broader discussion about the ways in which the events of the film fit within the Hundred Years' War, the relationship between France and England at the time, the Crusades, the slow rise of the French bourgeois, and religious reform. Louis XI oversaw many different transformations during his reign, some of which were precursors to the eventual dismantling of the French monarchy. Since the film depicts Louis XI as a despot, it is then worth asking students who among the French population might actually have resented the king for his initiatives and why.

Man of La Mancha (1972) interprets the mammoth seventeenth-century masterpiece *Don Quixote* very loosely. The narrative is structured as a "show within a show." That is, while in prison under the auspices of the Spanish Inquisition, the character of Cervantes must defend himself in a mock trial set up by his fellow inmates. His defense takes the form of a play, in which a mad old man called Alonso Quijana renames himself Don Quixote and goes off to seek adventure.

While certainly the entirety of the film can be shown, if short on time, simply screening the open scene of *Man of La Mancha* is likely sufficient for a unit on the Spanish Inquisition. The film opens with Cervantes at a festival staging a satirical play about the Spanish Inquisition. The performance leads to his arrest, imprisonment, and a performance of the song "Man of La Mancha."

The Tribunal of the Holy Office of the Inquisition was instituted in 1478 and was not officially disbanded until 1834, although its most active years were circa 1480 through 1530. Its geographic reach of its authority was similarly expansive, including not only Spain but also all of its territories. In contrast, *Man of La Mancha* is very small in scale, with an emphasis on a few key characters, and it takes place during the late sixteenth century over a limited period of time. The film does not explicitly engage with the central issue that concerned the Spanish Inquisition: the purity of the Catholic Church. Rather, in terms of ideology, the film—a product of the long 1960s—is more concerned about how authorities can infringe on personal freedoms than it is with religious doctrine.

The focus of *Man of La Mancha* on personal liberty, and how it chooses to frame the Inquisition, certainly provides ample room for discussions on popular-culture representations of the Inquisition more broadly, such as the ways in which such representations often ignore how the Inquisition targeted Jews and Muslims. Popular representations also present a relatively static version of the Inquisition, an issue that raises questions about how historians categorize and label events, such as "the Inquisition" or "the Age of Discoveries," that were long lived, covered a diverse geographical area, or both. Students should be asked, in what ways do conventional labels, as well as periodization, obscure historical realities and limit our understanding of them? In what ways are such labels useful for cultivating an understanding of history?

Given the emphasis of *Man of La Mancha*, it is also worth discussing the changing role of religion, religious organizations, and more particularly the Catholic Church, in society over time. One way to initiate a discussion about these changes is to ask why *Man of La Mancha* would opt to generally downplay the religious aspects of the Inquisition and what other charges Cervantes might have been charged with by the Inquisition in Spain during the seventeenth century. How might those charges have been investigated, and what sort of punishments would the character have had to endure? What might the differences have been if he had been a colonial subject or if the time frame were shifted forward or backward in time?[10]

ENLIGHTENMENT (CA. 1650–CA. 1800)

The inclusion of the film *Amadeus* (1984), a heavily fictionalized biography of Wolfgang Amadeus Mozart, adapted from the play by the same name, like the inclusion of *Monty Python and the Holy Grail*, might be stretching the definition of a musical rather far. However, Mozart's music is in many ways the point of the film. Everything from his works for the piano to his operas are heavily featured in ways that help to advance the film's plot and develop its two main characters, Wolfgang Amadeus Mozart and the man who perceives himself to be his rival, Antonio Salieri. As a representation of mid- to late eighteenth-century life and society in Europe, especially regarding life at court and popular culture, the film has much to recommend it. The film can be used to establish the wider cultural and social contexts for the Enlightenment. However, *Amadeus* is also a very long film featuring classical music— not a genre typically embraced by college students—and therefore using segments of the film within the class, rather than its entirety, is recommended. Of course, it is always possible to make the film (or indeed any other) available for students to view independently; quizzes tailored to the visual content of the film as well as specific historical facts are one way to ensure that students view it. If this method is used, it is important to then reinforce specific content areas by screening short snippets in class as discussion prompts.[11]

When using *Amadeus* in the classroom, it is important to recognize that it is a highly fictionalized version of Salieri and of his perceptions of Mozart. The film begins and ends with Salieri; it is his musings on the cruel workings of God that fuel the narrative. Although Salieri rejects God, he is hardly an Enlightenment figure, and indeed in many ways he represents an embedded, older model of understanding political and social authority. However, because Salieri narrates the action as he looks back on his life, *Amadeus* can serve as a way to discuss the nature of biography, autobiography, and historical narrative. It is worth asking students why certain historical figures are studied more than others. These types of questions can lead to a discussion concerning microhistory, and the ways in which unknown figures can be used to better understand larger issues and ideas within a particular historical period. As the film points out, while there was only one Mozart, there are thousands of Salieris in the world whose stories are generally ignored.

There are multiple scenes within *Amadeus* that provide insights into eighteenth-century court life, politics, nationalism, and popular culture, fashion, and religion. Approximately twenty minutes into the film, Mozart's music is performed for his patron the archbishop at a social gathering. This scene then transitions into a discussion Emperor Joseph II is having with his advisors regarding how to poach Mozart from his current patron, the archbishop. From there, the scene shifts to preparations for Mozart's visit to court, the presentation of the idea for his first commissioned opera, *The Abduction from the Seraglio*, and Mozart's performance of Salieri's piano march. Running at around fifteen minutes, the sequence imparts a large amount of information very quickly and takes considerable unpacking. The relationships between the courts of the archbishop and the emperor, between Germans and Italians, Germans and Turks, between royals and commoners, and God and man, are all referenced. This one sequence can be used as part of a larger conversation regarding European imperialism, power, and politics.

If using the film as a lens into Enlightenment thinking specifically, another suitable segment falls around an hour and thirty minutes into the film. In a relatively short scene, Mozart defends his use of the court-banned play *The Marriage of Figaro* as the basis for his newest opera. While courtiers insist that the older stories of gods and legends are more proper topics for art, Mozart argues for the power of music and common, relatable stories. In the spirit of the Enlightenment, Mozart challenges accepted dogma and authority figures with a well-articulated argument. Certainly Mozart himself was no Enlightenment figure—and some music historians argue that he was one of the first Romantics—but the scene can be used to tease out those differences and the ways in which Enlightenment thinking manifested itself.

1800s–1900s

Although *The Congress Dances* (1932) is primarily a bedroom farce, complete with a look-alike of Czar Alexander I, it engages with an important moment in European history: the Congress of Vienna and the Hundred Days (1814–1815). A gathering of the powers of Europe in the immediate aftermath of the Napoleonic Wars, the Congress of Vienna reorganized Europe to ensure a weaker France. Simultaneously, representatives from Russia, Prussia, Austria, and Great Britain all attempted to ensure that no one country would obtain more territory, or more power, than the other. It is a period when ideas of nationalism and nation were still very much in flux, with new political boundaries redrawn without much thought to who lived within those borders or how they might identify themselves. The musical, of course, only addresses these issues glancingly and instead frames the Congress of Vienna as being primarily a discussion about what to do with Napoleon Bonaparte, and the various machinations that take place in order to ensure that the Russian Czar misses the meeting at which Napoleon's fate will be decided.[12] Featuring Conrad Veidt as the scheming Prussian Prince Metternich, Czar Alexander I is primarily distracted by a beautiful shopgirl (Lilian Harvey), a lavish ball, and a wine garden. In the end, the romance between Czar and the shopgirl is ended when Napoleon escapes from his prison on Elba Island, and Alexander must return home to ensure Russia's safety.

An early musical, and based in the European operetta tradition, it is doubtful that *The Congress Dances* will appeal very much to students. However, its use and representation of Metternich, Alexander, and Napoleon can serve as the basis for students' own investigations into the biographies of these figures in a manner similar to how they dealt with historical figures featured in *Jupiter's Darling*. Indeed, the fact that both films elected to include fictional female characters as romantic interests for the fictionalized male historical characters can once again raise the issue of the presence, and absence, of women in standard histories. Further, the film's simplification of the actual political concerns of the Congress of 1815, while still taking great pains to represent the particular characteristics of different nations, can be used in several ways. First, as a German production, the representations can point students to the brewing European tensions of the 1930s that led to World War II. Second, the oversimplification of the historical record lends itself very well to broader discussions regarding the nature of historical knowledge, the role of popular culture in perpetuating certain kinds of historical knowledge, and the kinds of choices every historian must make in order to say anything legible about the past.

Like *Amadeus*, *Les Miserables* (2012) is a very long film, likely too long for it to be screened in its entirety during a normal class period. It is also a highly melodramatic and emotional film, and in that regard it can sweep

students along and potentially prevent them from fully deploying their ana-
lytical skills. Although any film can be an immersive experience for students,
Les Miserables works very hard to pull at the heart strings, something that is
characteristic of the European-style stage "megamusical" from which the
film is adapted.

Les Miserables spans the years from 1815 through the 1832 June Rebellion in Paris, France. The hero of the film is Jean Valjean. A poor man, he
was sent to prison for stealing bread, and while out on parole, the kindness of
a bishop changes his bitter perspective. As a result he resolves to craft a new
life, but to do so he must break parole and thus becomes a hunted man.
Valjean is hounded by Inspector Javert, who believes so passionately in the
purity of the law that he cannot understand anyone who would break even the
smallest of rules.

A common mistake that students will make regarding this film is that it is
about the French Revolution (1789–1799). It is very hard to shake students of
this assumption, even though the film declares the year right at the start and
makes it clear that the revolution is decades in the past. For this reason, the
Disney animated musical *The Hunchback of Notre Dame* (1996), which covers roughly the same period as *Les Miserables* without the conflation with
the revolution, might serve as a reasonable substitute. At ninety-one minutes,
The Hunchback of Notre Dame is also considerably shorter than *Les Miserables* and might be preferable for that reason alone. However, it is also good
pedagogy to push students to consider why they are conflating the two time
periods and to emphasize the ways in which survey courses construct the
historiography of France in particular, and Europe in general. What other
events, similar to the June Rebellion, are overlooked and why?

Although quite different in terms of their plots, both *The Hunchback of
Notre Dame* and *Les Miserables* have their roots in the novels of Victor
Hugo and are thus thematically similar to one another. They both cover
religion, redemption, forgiveness, social inequality, and the hypocrisy of the
law.[13] While *The Hunchback of Notre Dame* makes no reference to the June
Rebellion or the revolution, it can certainly be used as a means of exploring
key issues in French history. Class tensions and the complex relationships
between the Catholic Church and French politics are obvious starting points.

Having students read brief, one- to two-page excerpts from Hugo's novels
that align with particular moments in either film is one means through which
students can engage in a close textual reading with a source and to consider
what kind of source it is. How can fiction be used as historical evidence?
Should fiction be used as evidence for historical events and people, and if so,
what are some of the dangers and benefits of doing so? What sort of contextual research must be done when novels or other words of fiction are used in
practicing history? What can fiction teach historians about the craft of writing and narrative? These types of questions of course harken back to Hayden

White and his theories concerning the historical imagination and narrative, and are ways of helping students to seriously consider historical writing as a methodology.

Implicitly, both films engage with the long-term aftermath of the French Revolution on society and must be framed in that way. One way to do this is to note that the revolutionaries of the French Revolution won their fight and overthrew a government. Those involved in the June Rebellion in the nineteenth century lost their battle. Having students investigate why the first rebellion succeeded and the second rebellion failed enables them to synthesize multiple strands of information. Similar to the kinds of counterfactual exercises that ask "what would have been needed to enable the Confederacy to win the American Civil War?" placing the June Rebellion against the French Revolution puts the latter into a wider historical perspective. Students must consider, and then support and justify, why they view certain factors as more relevant than others, and how those factors contributed to the success or failure of the particular social movement.

Much of *Les Miserables* is concerned with Valjean's personal journey, and while very powerful, in the interest of time and focus, using excerpts from the film, especially its latter half, can be very effective. The film is neatly divided between the 1815 section covering Valjean's early life and the 1832 section in Paris, which focuses on the build up to, execution of, and aftermath from the rebellion. Starting with the "1832" half of the film does not require much groundwork to be laid for the students to grasp the basic plot and characters. There are several sequences from which to choose in order to illuminate the social and class inequalities within French (and European) society that drove upheaval and revolution; "Look Down" (the Beggars' Song) which opens the 1832 half of the film concisely lays out those inequalities.

Although in any musical the lyrics are always important, the lyrics to "Look Down" should be highlighted. The character Gavroche explicitly references the French Revolution and how little has changed over the years since the revolution. Visually, the sequence efficiently sets up the differences among the rich, the poor, and the university students who have allied themselves with the poor, and raises questions about who, exactly, in France and Europe were rising up against monarchies. When textbooks refer to "the people" in such uprisings, what does that actually mean? *Les Miserables* also questions why oppressed people might or might not choose to engage in political protest and what cross-class alliances can look like. Because university students are some of the primary protagonists in this half of the film, links can also be made to the student protests of the 1960s, as well as more contemporary social issues directly relevant to the students in the course.

Although a relatively unimportant moment in the grand scheme of French history, one scene of *Les Miserables* is useful to screen in order to highlight the cliché that truth is often quite stranger than fiction. Around an hour and five minutes into the film, as the time frame shifts from 1815 to 1832, the film depicts a gigantic, hollow elephant sculpture in the middle of the Bastille Square from which a squadron of street urchins emerges. It looks far too outlandish to be anything but a fabrication on the part of the filmmakers, but in fact the Elephant of the Bastille was conceived in 1808 and stood in the Bastille from 1813 to 1846. As a "fun fact" the existence of the statue can pique student interest, but it also ties back to Napoleon's reign and can be used for a discussion about public memorialization of events, the changing physical landscape of cities, and how material culture and architecture can serve as historical evidence.

Shifting from nineteenth-century France to Victorian England, thanks to the works of Charles Dickens, there are several musical films from which to choose when covering this period in history. That these films deal with issues of poverty and class conflict helps to create links to similar issues regarding the history of France, and of Europe more broadly during the nineteenth century. The *Muppet Christmas Carol* (1992) is a surprisingly faithful adaptation of Dickens's novel that directly confronts economic disparity. It also illustrates Victorian-era discourse idealizing women, children, and families.[14] *Oliver!* covers similar ground and, in the character of Fagin, touches on issues of anti-Semitism. For a more explicit representation of life in Victorian-era London, the 2007 musical *Sweeney Todd* can serve as a contrast to Dickens. The film, based on the musical of the same name, is rooted in a popular (and much-adapted) 1840s Victorian penny-dreadful novel. Placing Dickens's Christian moralizing alongside the murderous solutions to economic disparities and social injustice as presented in *Sweeney Todd* neatly encompasses how the discourse of Victorian England was variously interpreted by contemporaries.

Following the highly London-centric views of the Victorian era, it is important to connect the domestic sphere with the colonial sphere. *The King and I* (1956) takes place during the late 1860s in Siam, and while it is an American view of British imperialism—and a very benign view—it nonetheless helps to make clear the ways in which domestic and foreign policies were intimately connected through the character of the teacher Anna Leonowens. The power of *The King and I* lies precisely in the ways in which it romanticizes the process of colonial rule. Although there are multiple moments of cultural misunderstandings throughout the film, the number "Getting to Know You," which takes place in a classroom in front of a world map, highlights the ways in which imperial rule was justified as a civilizing force for "lesser races."

1900s

With the turn of the twentieth century, the volume of historical and social change increases at a dizzying pace. Thus, with one or two exceptions, using films that highlight broad themes and issues, rather than specific historical events, is generally more sustainable within the context of a survey course.

Although it does not explicitly reference the Russian Revolution by name, *Fiddler on the Roof* (1971), which is set in the Russian Ukraine in 1905, implicitly addresses the tensions that led to the march on the Winter Palace in St. Petersburg, as well as the immediate aftermath of that event. Set in the small town of Anatevka, like the majority of musicals discussed throughout this book, the film focuses on the individual lives of a small group of people rather than large-scale historical events. Specifically, the film is about the Tevye family, a Jewish family comprised of five daughters, the wife/mother, and a husband/father who must negotiate the ways in which both his family and his country are changing. The Jewish faith and what it means to the family, the community, and eventually to the Russian Empire is pivotal to the narrative. That said, much of the film is only concerned with the Tevye family; larger historical concerns are viewed at the microlevel. This limited lens is even apparent at the end of the film when the Jews are forced to leave Anatevka by the Russian Christians. For issues concerning the shape of the Russia Empire prior to World War I, the Pale of Settlement, European anti-Semitism, and the Jewish diaspora, *Fiddler on the Roof* opens up many areas of discussion as well as laying the groundwork for discussions about World War II.[15]

Given the focus of *Fiddler on the Roof* on the family and the need for a relatively large cast, high schools very often produce a version of the stage show, and as a result, many students may well be familiar with it. It is also often the case that *Fiddler on the Roof* within high school settings is used as a means of opening up discussions regarding the Jewish religion and tradition.

With a running time of three hours, and with its focus on family melodrama as well as the Jewish tradition, segments of the film can be shown. There are three musical sequences that lay out the historically strained relationships between Jews and Christians: the opening number "Tradition"; the wedding of Tzeitel and Motel; and the end sequence when the Jews are forced to leave Anatevka. "Tradition" introduces the tenuous balance between Jews and Christians in Anatevka, as well as the cultural and religious practices that set the Jewish part of town apart. Lyrically, the song is quite explicit about what makes the Jewish people different and allows for discussion about why and how those differences mattered prior to and during the twentieth century. It can also raise issues of the ways in which Russia constructed itself as a nation, and since the scene ends with the introduction of Perchik—a young Jewish Marxist—wider political concerns can also be discussed.

The wedding of Tzeitel and Motel is justly famous for its "bottle dance" scene, and if there is time it is certainly worth showing the wedding sequence in its entirety. The emotional import of the destruction wrought by the Russian soldiers that occurs at the height of the celebrations will have that much more resonance. The event is the embodiment of a pogrom, and the film makes it clear that such events were not random explosions of ethnic/religious tensions but were instead political tools with the force of government behind them. Having student trace the history of the pogrom back to the nineteenth century and forward through the mid-twentieth century lays clear groundwork for the events of World War II. It can also create important links between the distant and the more recent past, such as the ethnic cleansing in former Yugoslavia.[16]

If *Monty Python and the Holy Grail* was used earlier in the semester, create a timeline of the social forces that led to Marx, the Revolution of 1905, and the Revolution of 1917. As with *Les Miserables*, which at first blush seems to be about the French Revolution but is not, *Fiddler on the Roof* is set during a lesser-known revolutionary period. Both films thus highlight the ongoing nature of class (and religious) conflict within Europe. They can emphasize the ways in which major events such as the French Revolution and the Russian Revolution had precursors and aftermaths that are just as important in understanding the shape of European history.

Again, depending on time, the entire end sequence as the Jewish population prepares to, and then leaves, Anatevka can be shown. If part of the intent is to give students a clearer sense of the scope of the Jewish diaspora, screening the ending sequence in its entirety is very effective. An effective project is to have students research migration and population trends in Europe and to use the places named by the various characters as starting points. The issues of internal and external migration, and the forces that trigger such population shifts among particular ethnic and religious groups, is poignantly illustrated. Alternatively, the three- to four-minute clip of the song "Anatevka" can be screened in order to provide a baseline for discussion regarding the Jewish diaspora, with the same assignment attached.[17]

A good transitional film from the turn of the twentieth century to the more modern era of history is the little-known *Balalaika* (1939). The film begins in Russia in 1914, just prior to the Russian Revolution, and ends in Paris of the 1920s. It is primarily a star vehicle for Nelson Eddy. However, *Balalaika* works to help shift focus from Russia to the First World War and then to the 1920s. It also further emphasizes the significance of Russia/the Soviet Union to European and world history, and previews many of the issues that will become important during the Cold War. The music for the film is an interesting mélange of preexisting songs and compositions; very little was composed specifically for it. Eddy's character, a Russian prince, falls in love with a cabaret singer, whose father is involved with the Reds and who takes part in the assassination of the prince's father. Father and daughter are exiled to Siberia just prior to the start of World War I, with the prince winding up on the Austro-Russian border during the war before he eventually emigrates to Paris, where the two lovers are finally reunited.

The film clearly romanticizes revolution and war, although a scene on the front lines with enemies singing "Silent Night" in tandem before the battle begins is very effective. *Balalaika* serves to open up more discussions regarding the politics of the Russian Revolution, nostalgia for the tsars, and the impact of World War I. It thus serves as a good companion to *Fiddler on the Roof* and as way to transition to *Oh! What a Lovely War* (1969) and its much more bitter, and realistic, interpretation of the First World War.

While the majority of musical films in this book were adapted from fictional—or highly fictionalized—source materials, *Oh! What a Lovely War*, an unlikely sounding British musical about World War I, is grounded in primary sources. Not only are the songs performed in the film those that were sung by troops during the war, but also a significant portion of the dialogue in the film is lifted directly from published diaries and letters of generals, politicians, and common soldiers. The film is also valuable in that it covers the entirety of the war from 1914 through Armistice Day and thus tracks the ways in which attitudes and ideas about the war changed.

When screening the film, it must be made clear that it was produced in 1969, a time when antiwar feelings regarding Vietnam were running high, even in Europe. It is certainly possible, depending on the timeline for the course, to lay the groundwork for a future discussion regarding Vietnam and the political turmoil of the 1960s and 1970s.

Oh! What a Lovely War has a clear point of view manifested through satire and the juxtaposition of patriotic words with horrific imagery or dance production numbers that mock the speaker/singer. Leaders such as General Haig are relentlessly critiqued—not without cause—but the film cannot therefore be viewed as neutral or objective in how it uses primary sources.

There is value in the film's polemical position from a teaching and learning perspective. First, the mockery directed toward those leaders who lead men into war serves as a very effective segue into the disillusionment and modernism of 1920s Europe. Second, and perhaps more important, *Oh! What a Lovely War* reveals how arguments can be supported using primary sources and reinforces the idea that history as a discipline does not just present the facts but also interprets those facts to create a narrative. It is highly recommended that students be given excerpts from the many primary sources used in the film to read prior to the screening. Including song lyrics and speeches, students should be asked to analyze the documents in terms of what they reveal about the war and about the authors of the documents. After screening the film, ask students to reanalyze those materials; how did their understanding of a particular document change as a result of how it was represented in the film? After the film screening, it can also be fruitful to have students examine World War I propaganda posters and to discuss ideas concerning patriotism and nation that the film critiques and that the posters embrace. Alternatively, if using a standard textbook in conjunction with the film, have students debate the value of "neutrality" when it comes to representing the past or have them examine the precise language of the textbook itself. Does the textbook present a point of view, and if so, what is it?

Another, and highly problematic, film concerning the First World War is *The Golden Dawn*. Set in Africa, the film is primarily concerned with a white British soldier's love for an "African" woman, Dawn. It eventually transpires that Dawn was born of white parents and raised to believe she is African. Released in 1930 and adapted from the 1927 stage musical of the same name, the film is extraordinarily racist in its representations of Africa and Africans. The film is also, for want of a better term, quite creaky in its techniques and not particularly well crafted or acted. But even with these many caveats, *The Golden Dawn* does address the truly international scope of the war and demonstrates the colonial stakes that German and British military had in Africa. Have students examine a map of Africa before, during, and after the war. They can track the shifts of colonial power during the late nineteenth and early twentieth centuries in conjunction with the cavalier way in which the film handles the exchange of power over Africa from German to British commanders. Such an exercise helps students to understand how attitudes toward Africa and Africans shaped the process of, and justification for, colonialism as well as providing a space for a discussion about postcolonial views of World War I that moves beyond the traditional European narrative. Depending on the nature of the course, students could also read an excerpt of Robin D. G. Kelley's 1999 article "'But a Local Phase of a World Problem': Black History's Global Vision, 1883–1950," which creates a historiography of how generations of African American historians connected Africa to Europe in ways that white historians simply did not.[18] It is important, however, to reinforce for students that incorporating Africa and Africans within the scope of World War I is not a radical move.

As with the history of the United States, teaching a history of Western Civilization through musical films changes when the 1920s are reached. As noted in earlier chapters, with the advent of sound technologies, musical films were some of the earliest genre of films produced. In addition, the 1920s is a decade that is closely associated with new music and new technologies, and so musical film representations of the era are not particularly hard to come by. What can be difficult is finding musical films that articulate a view of the 1920s that is anything less than positive. While Europeans as a whole were suffering the aftermath of the First World War, musical films—which typically embrace utopian communities—rarely reflected the painful realities of life in Europe after the First World War.

The beginning of World War II, however, is a very different story, a fact made apparent in two highly divergent films: *Cabaret* (1972) and *The Sound of Music* (1965). *Cabaret* is a highly cynical film set in 1930s Germany and filled with unlikable characters. It also incorporates bisexuality and abortion within its plot line in ways that may further complicate how students receive it. However, its explicit commentary on anti-Semitism, the depiction of the conflict between the Nazi and the Communist parties in Germany, and its inclusion of the ways in which German citizens were complicit in—or at least deliberately ignorant about—the rise of Adolf Hitler make the film as a whole well worth screening. In contrast, *The Sound of Music*, loosely based on the true story of the Van Trapp family who escaped the Nazi regime in Austria, avoids any direct mention of Jews. With its straightforward narrative, *The Sound of Music* rejects cynicism and hopelessness.

While *The Sound of Music*, with its famous score and emphasis on the family, will likely be quite well known to students, *Cabaret* may or may not be a musical they know, thus it can be very fruitful to pair scenes of the film together. Juxtaposing how characters in *Cabaret* view the Nazis against how the characters in *The Sound of Music* view the Nazis helps to defamiliarize the latter film. It raises the question of the ways in which popular culture representations of the Nazis as villains ignores much of the history behind the Nazis as a political force in Germany and how the devastation of the First World War helped to lead to the second. The juxtaposition of the two films further serves to open up a discussion regarding how and why the Nazis rose to power and the complex question of why the Nazi political party was embraced by so many Germans.

The lack of any commentary on Jews and Judaism in *The Sound of Music*, in contrast to the subplot in *Cabaret* involving the impossibility of marriage between a Christian man and a Jewish woman, can also be used in class to highlight the plight of Jewish people just before, during, and after the war. Why did Hitler target Jewish people in particular for his "final solution"? Why, as evidenced by the absence of Jews from *The Sound of Music*, did it take so long for the scale and scope of the Holocaust to be recognized?[19]

As noted in previous chapters, the popularity of film musicals began to wane during the late 1950s and 1960s. Musicals set in those decades are often cheap teen rock musicals. While such films represent specific cultural moments, they rarely address concrete historical issues, events, or people. Specific issues need to be addressed more thematically and, to a certain extent, from the side rather than straight on. For example, the 1950s saw the rise of the decolonization movement across various European empires, but there are few musicals that deal explicitly with the topic. Other central issues for Europe after World War II, and for which it is relatively easy to find musical films, include the rebuilding of Europe after the war, the rise of Communism, and the Cold War. As with musicals that address the history of the United States post World War II, the choices available for use regarding the history of Europe are relatively limited and become more limited as the decades move forward. This does not mean that musical films should not be used, but it does mean that one must be even more imaginative in using them within the classroom, with the focus less on specific events and more on cultural shifts and social moods.

An example of a musical film not typically thought of as being "about" postwar Europe is *An American in Paris* (1951). Better known for the spectacular seventeen-minute ballet number featuring stars Gene Kelly (as Jerry) and Leslie Caron (as Lise), the film is set in postwar Paris and is quite explicit about its time frame. One of the central obstacles between the romance of American ex-patriot and World War II veteran Jerry and Paris native Lise is that Lise feels obligated to marry a secondary character named Henri because he kept her safe during the German occupation of Paris. Although never made explicit, the idea that America is helping to renew Europe, and Paris in particular, runs throughout the film.[20]

The number "I Got Rhythm" exemplifies the idea that Americans are in Europe to educate and renew Europe. Kelly, shifting between French and English, teaches some English to a group of French children he has befriended. Before the number starts, the children clamor after Jerry asking for chewing gum, a hint of wartime deprivation, continued shortages, and American generosity. During the number itself, he mimes different popular culture figures, including Hopalong Cassidy, for the children to identify. Within the structure of the film, "I Got Rhythm" solidifies Jerry as a good and likable person, but within the context of a conversation on the rebuilding of postwar Europe, the excerpt can be used to prompt students to consider the ways in which Europe was forced to become reliant on the United States and the different perceptions regarding that help. Understandably, *An American in Paris* provides a very American-centric view, but what might alternative perceptions be, and how might those differences inflect international relationships over time?

As scholars of the film musical have noted, in contrast to the 1940s, few American musicals made during the 1950s directly addressed contemporary issues. *Silk Stockings* is an exception. A remake of the Greta Garbo star vehicle *Ninotchka* (1939), *Silk Stockings* involves an American film producer (Fred Astaire) trying to hire a Russian film composer to score his new film. Set in Paris, the composer decides to stay in the West, which means that Russian operatives are sent out to bring him back home.[21] The film very clearly lays out the perceived differences between Soviet and American/ Western ways, using music and choreography as the means to do so. Several numbers, including "We Can't Go Back to Moscow," "All of You," and "Siberia" exemplify ideas about repressive Soviet, and open Western, cultures. Have students engage in close readings of these numbers to unpack the

(American) cultural assumptions embedded within them, especially in terms of how gender and a romantic narrative are used to represent national differences.[22]

Shifting gears away from the obvious tensions of the Cold War is the British pseudo-documentary about the Beatles, *A Hard Day's Night* (1964). Not only does the film represent Cold War culture through the popular culture phenomenon that was the Beatles, but also it does so from a British perspective at a time when the British class system was changing and intergenerational tensions were high. For American students, the film also highlights how memories of World War II lingered in England and Europe in ways that it did not in the United States. In an early nonmusical scene set on a train, the band members share a compartment with a middle-aged businessman who, tiring of their antics, snaps "I fought the war for your sort!" Asking the students to articulate the different meanings behind "your sort" is a good starting point for understanding these cultural shifts.

If there is sufficient time, an excellent exercise is to have students create a timeline of important events in European history during the 1960s.[23] Working either in groups or individually, what makes this exercise unique is its use of the career highlights of the Beatles as the initial historical markers around which the broader timeline can be built. There are many variations on this assignment. Students can focus exclusively on British history, or different students/groups of students can be assigned different countries from which a final, course-wide timeline can be compiled. With improved radio technology, record production, and institutionalization of television sets within people's homes, the Beatles were an international phenomenon and demonstrate the rise of a global popular culture. Mapping crucial European events onto a timeline of important events with the career of the Beatles forces students to make determinations about what is deemed valuable historical information. In the age of popular culture websites such as Buzzfeed.com, which mix investigative reporting into police brutality alongside "top ten" lists concerning cute cat pictures, the assignment reflects the ways in which students are already engaging with current events and models a way of thinking through the distinctions between types of events.

Continuing with the British theme, and admittedly skimming over the 1970s, is the dance-heavy film *Billy Elliot* (2000). The film is set during the 1984–1985 coal miner's strike and can usefully be paired with *Brassed Off* (1996), which is set ten years after the end of the strike action depicted in *Billy Elliot*. Both films depict the changing place of coal in postindustrial England, the rise of the Conservative government, and the long-term, material impacts those technological and political shifts had on a particular segment of the British population. Arguably, both films stretch the definition of what is meant by a musical. However, *Billy Elliot* focuses on the titular character's desire to be a dancer, while *Brassed Off* concerns a brass wind ensemble comprised of miners who are struggling to maintain the group in the face of another wave of pit closures and town strife. Both films contain one of the crucial elements of a musical (or dansical) film: when Billy and the characters in *Brassed Off* cannot adequately express their feelings verbally, they do so using performance.

While specific to the coal miners and to British politics, both films can be usefully deployed to discuss broader economic and political trends in Europe during the 1980s. As has often been suggested with other films discussed in this book, assign the students to compare and contrast the coal miners' strikes in England with similar actions in other countries at the same time. What economic and technological shifts were occurring that meant that coal was no longer a profitable resource? What, if anything, took the place of coal? Why did unions—or unions within certain industries—lose much of their political clout during the 1980s? How did figures such as Margaret Thatcher represent the miners in her political speeches, and how did the miners and the unions attempt to counter her rhetoric? Both films also once again raise the issue of the effectiveness of the arts to effect change and how widespread that change needs to be before students might consider it effective.

CONCLUSION

Unfortunately, there are few European or American film musicals that specifically address late twentieth-century European history. The fall of the Berlin Wall, the conflict in former Yugoslavia, and many other seminal events are not touched. As noted in earlier chapters, one solution to this problem is to ask students why film musicals do not address these events. Is it the case that not enough time and distance from the events has passed to allow for a film in the vein of *Oh! What a Lovely War* to be produced about the end of the Cold War? Is it that these events are too complex to set to music? Is it simply that musical films are no longer profitable to produce? All of these questions go to issues of historical knowledge and the process of producing history.

NOTES

1. The term "absent presence" comes from the theorist Jacques Derrida.
2. Although Japan is not typically viewed as having a film culture that would embrace, much less produce, musicals, there is in fact a substantial body of film musicals made in Japan dating back to the 1930s. Michael Baskett, *The Attractive Empire: Transnational Film Culture in Imperial Japan* (Honolulu: University of Hawaii Press, 2008), 58–63.
3. It is also the case that many students taking history courses are doing so with an eye to becoming secondary or elementary school teachers, and thus at the college level, certain areas of content coverage are expected or mandated in order to meet state certification requirements for teachers.

4. Esther Williams begin her career as a competitive swimmer, and the majority of films in which she starred managed to work swimming into the plot in some fashion.

5. An outlier to this pattern, *The Court Jester* (1955), while well worth watching, ignores any connections to English history or legend and would be a difficult fit within a history course.

6. The 2009 film *Vision: From the Life of Hildegard von Bingen*, a biography of the German Benedictine nun (and composer), while an interesting meditation on the role of women in religion during the medieval era, contains even less singing than *Monty Python and the Holy Grail* and thus does not fit within the rubric of this book.

7. Dale Larsen, *A Book about the Film* Monty Python and the Holy Grail*: All the References from African Swallows to Zoot* (Lanham, MD: Rowman & Littlefield, 2015).

8. Another version of the film was produced in 1930 but is not available on DVD. The 1956 version is more easily available on DVD and through online streaming services.

9. David Georgi's 2013 translation of Villon's poems is a good resource. Francois Villon, *Poems*, trans. David Georgi (Evanston, IL: Northwestern University Press, 2013).

10. As with *Monty Python and the Holy Grail*, *Man of La Mancha* focuses on the partnership between a nobleman and a peasant. Another through line for the course could be the changing, or static, nature of class relationships in Europe.

11. Students can take five minutes to Google a film and read its synopsis on multiple websites. Thus, it is important that quizzes target material in the film that would be difficult to know unless it had been viewed at least once.

12. A German film, *The Congress Dances* was filmed in German, French, and English. Eric Rentschler, *The Use and Abuse of Cinema: German Legacies from the Weimar Era to the Present* (New York: Columbia University Press, 2015), 123–27.

13. The also cover unrequited love.

14. Miss Piggy portrays the character of Mrs. Cratchit, who is one of the primary examples of ideal womanhood; this might give some pause.

15. As with many of the films dealt with in this chapter, class tensions also play a role in the film. Tevye is very poor, and his poverty, and how it impacts his relationship to his daughters, is crucial to the film's narrative.

16. Mapping out the history of the pogroms can also involve mapping the history of the Pale of Settlement from the eighteenth century forward and noting the ways in which the history and the geography intersect.

17. Because the musical is based on the short stories by author Sholem Aleichem about the character of Tevye, it is of course also appropriate to have students read excerpts from those works of fiction as well.

18. Robin D. G. Kelley, "'But a Local Phase of a World Problem': Black History's Global Vision, 1883–1950," *Journal of American History* 86, no. 3 (1999): 1045–77.

19. If one is willing to stretch the meaning of the term "musical film," *The Pianist* (2002) is a historical film based on the memoir of the Polish-Jewish pianist Wladyslaw Szpilman and heavily features classical music as played by Szpilman.

20. Gerald Mast, *Can't Help Singin'* (New York: Overlook, 1987), 260.

21. Including *Silk Stockings* in a course focusing on European history might be considered a stretch, especially as the film is very much from an American point of view, with Europe as the backdrop.

22. For a close reading of some of the historical gendered assumptions embedded with *Silk Stockings* and how representations of gender reflect ideas about national identity, see Helen Laville, "'Our Country Endangered by Underwear': Fashion, Femininity, and the Seduction Narrative in *Ninotchka* and *Silk Stockings*," *Diplomatic History* 30, no. 4 (September 2006): 623–44.

23. There are numerous free timeline applications available online, some which also include a mapping component so that time and place can mapped; myHistro, http://www.myhistro.com, is one such example, but there are many others.

DOCUMENTS

Sample Syllabus

Note: The following sample syllabus is for the first half of a US history survey course (precontact through the American Civil War). There are many standard history textbooks for survey courses. Rather than advocate for any particular text (all of them have advantages and disadvantages), I am using *Generic History Textbook* as the placeholder.

HI 103: US HISTORY, PRECONTACT THROUGH THE CIVIL WAR—COURSE DESCRIPTION

This survey course provides an overview of the development and maturation of an Anglo-American society in the "New World" as well as an introduction to historical thinking and writing. The course stresses the interconnectedness of social, economic, and political history and the diversity of the American experience in the colonies and in the early republic by region, class, race, and gender. The course will use a combination of textbook readings and the screening of film musicals that address early American history as a means of promoting critical historical thinking.

REQUIRED READINGS

Smith, Sam. *Generic U.S. History Textbook: Precontact through the Civil War.*
Rampolla, Mary Lynn. *A Pocket Guide to Writing in History.* 8th ed. Boston: Bedford/St. Martin's, 2015.

STUDENT LEARNING OUTCOMES (SLOS)

A passing grade for this course signifies that a student has met the following objectives. Students will . . .

SLO	Assessment
Articulate key events, persons, trends, places, and dates in early American history.	• online discussions • quizzes • exam
Analyze relationships among different regional, social, ethnic, economic, and racial groups.	• in-class work (includes discussions, small-group work, etc.) • online discussion • group project • quizzes • exam
Examine the development of American governmental structures and processes.	• in-class work (includes discussions, small-group work, etc.) • online discussion • quizzes • exam
Analyze and apply the differences between primary and secondary sources.	• source analysis essays • annotated bibliography
Apply historical thinking.	• final project

WEEK 1: INTRODUCTION TO THE COURSE; PRIMARY AND SECONDARY SOURCES

Readings/Assignments

- Rampolla, chapter 2, "Working with Sources," *Pocket Guide*
- Forum discussion: Read over the syllabus. What is one aspect of early American history you are interested in learning more about, and why? What is one aspect of early American history you are not interested in learning more about, and why?

In Class

- *Hair* (1979): How can we tell the difference between primary and secondary sources? What criteria are applied?
- Quiz 1

WEEK 2: FIRST ENCOUNTERS AND BRITISH SETTLEMENT

Readings/Assignments

- Chapter 1, *Generic Textbook*
- Forum discussion: Compare/contrast the different kinds of "first contact" experienced by Europeans and Native peoples.

In Class

- *Pocahontas* (1995)
- Excerpts from John Smith's writings
- Group work: Compare and contrast Anglo-American views on Native Americans.
- Quiz 2

WEEK 3: LIFE, CULTURE, AND POLITICS

Readings/Assignments

- Chapter 2, *Generic Textbook*
- Rampolla, chapter 3, "Approaching Typical Assignments in History," *Pocket Guide*
- Forum discussion: How "British" were the colonists? How "American" were the colonists? What kinds of shifts occurred in these identities over time?

In Class

- Writing a single-source analysis paper (first source analysis is due next week!)
- Quiz 3

WEEK 4: ROAD(S) TO REVOLUTION

Readings/Assignments

- Chapter 3, *Generic Textbook*
- Forum discussion: What factors—events, cultural, geographic, economic, and demographic—fostered colonial unity prior to the American Revolution? What factors worked against colonial unity? Based on your understanding of these different factors working for and against colonial cohesion, was the American Revolution inevitable?
- First source analysis (a short primary reading) due

In Class

- *1776* (1972)
- Excerpts from loyalists and revolutionaries: "Rebellion: 1775–1776," American in Class, http://americainclass.org/. Small-group work: Mirroring the "Sit Down John" number from *1776*, your group should take the excerpts from loyalists and revolutionaries, select a musical style to represent each side, and rewrite the arguments into more contemporary language.
- Quiz 4

WEEK 5: ESTABLISHING A NEW NATION

Readings/Assignments

- Chapter 4, *Generic Textbook*
- Rampolla, chapters 6 and 7, "Plagiarism" and "Quoting and Documenting Sources," *Pocket Guide*
- Forum discussion: Adopt the position either of a Federalist or of an anti-Federalist, and make an argument for/against ratification of the Constitution. In your response post, reply to someone who holds the position opposite from your own and engage in a (friendly!) debate.

In Class

- *Gigi* (1958). "I Remember It Well." Understanding the importance of documenting your sources, framing your research questions, and the choices that are made in standard historical narratives. (Question: In the political history concerning the ratification of the Constitution, what other stories are left out?)

* Quiz 5

WEEK 6: THE JEFFERSONIAN REPUBLIC AND FEDERAL POWERS

Readings/Assignments

* Chapter 5, *Generic Textbook*
* Forum discussion: Was the election of 1800 truly revolutionary? Why or why not?
* Second source analysis (an image) due

In Class

* Group work on presentation for midterm
* Quiz 6

WEEK 7: MASS DEMOCRACY AND THE AGE OF JACKSON

Readings/Assignments

* Chapter 6, *Generic Textbook*
* Forum discussion: Within the context of the nineteenth century, who was "the common man"? Who was and who was not considered to be a "common man"?
* Third source analysis (a material object) due

In Class

* Group work on presentation for midterm
* Quiz 7

WEEK 8: GROUP PRESENTATIONS (IN LIEU OF MIDTERM)

In Class

* Presentations

WEEK 9: WORK, IMMIGRATION, AND RIGHTS

Readings/Assignments

- Chapter 7, *Generic Textbook*
- Rampolla, chapters 4 and 5, "Following Conventions of Writing in History" and "Writing a Research Paper," *Pocket Guide*
- Forum discussion: The nineteenth century was a time of great change. How did Americans variously engage with the concept that America was "exceptional"? In what ways did they express the "exceptional" nature of America?
- Fourth source analysis (journal article) due

In Class

- *The Shocking Miss Pilgrim* (1947). Group work: Although this film is set in 1874 and falls a bit outside of our timeline, it still addresses labor, gender roles, technology, and voting rights in the nineteenth century. Each group will respond to the film in terms of how it engages with one of these themes.
- Quiz 8

WEEK 10: INTERSECTIONS: SLAVERY AND MANIFEST DESTINY

Readings/Assignments

- Chapter 8, *Generic Textbook*
- Forum discussion: Many Americans in the nineteenth century believed that expansion across North America was "destined." Why did they believe this? Was westward expansion indeed inevitable? Why or why not?

In Class

- *Annie Get Your Gun* (1950). Group work: Think back to *Pocahontas* (1995), and compare/contrast the histories of the Powhatan people of New England to the tribes named in "I'm an Indian Too." How are popular culture representations of the relationships between Native Americans and white Americans different from the historical realities of those relationships?
- Quiz 9

WEEK 11: DEBATES: SLAVERY VERSUS ABOLITION

Readings/Assignments

- Chapter 9, *Generic Textbook*
- Forum discussion: How similar/different was the Compromise of 1850 to the Missouri Compromise of 1820? How did each sectional compromise affect the balance of power between North and South? What were the alternatives?
- Annotated bibliography due

In Class

- *The Littlest Rebel* (1935)
- Excerpt from George Fitzhugh's *Sociology of the South; or, the Failure of Free Society*, 1854.
- Free Soil Society Party Platform, 1848. Group work: Examine the arguments for and against slavery from the nineteenth and the early twentieth centuries. How persistent were such arguments, and why might that be the case?
- Quiz 10

WEEK 12: CIVIL WAR BEGINNINGS

Readings/Assignments

- Chapter 10, *Generic Textbook*
- Forum discussion: What was the most important factor/event/person without which the Civil War would not have happened? In other words, what was the "tipping point" that made the Civil War a certainty, and why, based on the evidence, do you think that is the case?

In Class

- Pair/share of final projects. What progress has been made since the annotated bibliography? Where do you need help?
- Quiz 11

WEEK 13: THE CIVIL WAR, PART 1

Readings/Assignments

- Chapter 11, *Generic Textbook*
- Forum discussion: Compare and contrast Lincoln and Davis as leaders, and the strengths/weaknesses of the Union and the Confederacy at the start of the war. Pretend you do not know what the outcome of the war will be: which side will win the war and why, based on your comparisons?

In Class

- Group work: an examination of Civil War photographs as historical evidence; excerpt from Ken Burns's television documentary *The Civil War*. We will also discuss how Burns uses music in his documentary in relationship to the musicals screened during the semester.
- Quiz 12

WEEK 14: THE CIVIL WAR, PART 2

Readings/Assignments

- Chapter 12, *Generic Textbook*
- Forum discussion: Ultimately, what was the Civil War about? Justify your response.
- Final source analysis (one of the screened films) due

In Class

- Group work: *The Littlest Rebel* (1935), Burns's documentary series, and Frederick Douglass's essay "Decoration Day" (1894) all make particular arguments about the history of the Civil War. What are those arguments? What kind of musical film could be made that would be reflective of the Frederick Douglass essay concerning that history?
- Quiz 13

WEEK 15: AFTERMATH AND RECONSTRUCTION

Readings/Assignments

- Chapter 13, *Generic Textbook*

- Forum discussion: What is one short-answer question that you would expect to see on the final exam? What would be the ideal answer to the question?
- Final research project due

In Class

- Group work: Create a study guide for the final exam. What are the key events, people, and concepts covered in the course?
- Quiz 14

FINALS WEEK

Assignments

In-class work (includes discussions, small-group work, etc.): During the semester, you will be expected to contribute to the in-class learning environment in a number of ways. This includes, but is not limited to, discussion, small-group work, and lightning presentations.

Online discussion: Each week you must contribute twice to the online discussion forum. Your first post—two hundred words minimum—must be in response to the question posted by the instructor. Your second response—one hundred words minimum—must be in response to a classmate and extend the intellectual engagement with the topic. Be advised that while writing "good post, I think you raise some nice points" is a polite thing to do, it does not demonstrate intellectual engagement with a topic. Such phrases will not be counted in the word count.

Group project presentation: In lieu of a midterm, students working in groups of four to five will create their own film musical version concerning an aspect of American history covered in the first half of the class. Students must provide a plot synopsis, a narrative outline, and a list of songs for the film. Additionally, students are required to justify what they decided to include and what they decided to exclude from their musicalization of history. For example, for a musical film version about the War of 1812, students should articulate why they elected to start the film in 1812 rather than with the trade restrictions of 1807. Your reasoning behind the song selections—what they add to the film in terms of understanding the history, understanding the characters, and so forth—must also be included. There will be time in class allotted to work on this assignment. Presentations should run ten min-

utes, and each member of the group must speak for at least two minutes during the presentation.

Source analysis essays: Over the duration of the semester, you will complete five short essays of three hundred words each. You will be asked
to analyze the following: one each of three different types of primary
sources (a short text, an image, or a material object); a short peer-
reviewed article from a scholarly journal; and a film of your choosing
that has been screened in class.

Annotated bibliography: To assist you in the completion of your final
research project (see below), you are required to complete an annotated bibliography. The bibliography must contain six secondary sources
(four of which must be from peer-reviewed, scholarly journals) and
two primary sources. All sources should be listed using *Chicago Manual of Style* format. The annotations should run fifty to a hundred
words. You must include a two-hundred-word introduction to the bibliography that briefly explains your research question and the historical scope for your project. You may reuse the sources selected as part
of the source analysis essays, but as part of the annotation, the sources
must be placed in the context of your final research project. In other
words, you cannot simply recycle your "source analysis essays" for
the annotations.

Final Project

You may select either option 1 or option 2.

Option 1: A Formal Research Paper

The research paper is a refinement and expansion of your research proposal
that formed the basis of your annotated bibliography. It is the final, formal
written presentation of your research and argument. The goal of this assignment is for you to demonstrate your ability to recognize and analyze key
events, ideas, or individuals that have shaped US history. The paper should
conform to the *Chicago Manual of Style* using twelve-point Times New
Roman font, double spaced, with regular, one-inch margins. The paper must
consist of five to seven full pages of text, excluding the (nonannotated)
bibliography listing the sources used, which does not figure into the page
count. By "five full pages" I do not mean four pages plus one paragraph on
the fifth page.

Option 2: A Media Presentation

The media presentation is a refinement and expansion of your research proposal that formed the basis of your annotated bibliography. It is the final,

formal presentation of your research and argument. The goal of this assignment is for you to demonstrate your ability to recognize and analyze key events, ideas, or individuals that have shaped US history. You must record your voice-over as part of a PowerPoint, Prezi, Keynote, or other presentation app such as Explain Everything or iMovie to create a ten- to twelve-minute presentation on your research and argument (roughly the equivalent of a five- to seven-page written paper). If you select this option, you must still include a final slide that contains a (nonannotated) list of the academic, scholarly sources used as the foundation for your projects. The bibliography must conform to *Chicago Manual of Style* format. Please note that similar to a research paper, this is not something you will show to the whole class.

Quizzes: Each week, there will be a short, objective quiz designed to test your knowledge of the readings.

Exam: At the end of the semester, there will be a final, cumulative exam. The exam will have three components. The first is the objective section, based on the weekly quizzes. The second is a series of targeted short-answer questions related to our online discussion forums. The last section is a more broadly framed essay question that will have you synthesize information and concepts related to early American history.

Musicals for the Classroom

The following list summarizes musical films mentioned or discussed in the text, along with a few others omitted for reasons of space and flow. The year (and, if not the United States, country) of release are noted for the sake of context; and the running time, as an aid to scheduling. The Motion Picture Association of America (MPAA) rating is included—when applicable—for readers whose institutional culture makes the use of R-rated films in the classroom problematic. Cast, crew, and production information, readily available from the Internet Movie Database and similar reference sources, are not included.

Across the Universe (2007; rated PG-13; 133 minutes). Using the Beatles song catalog and set during the late 1960s through the early 1970s, the film focuses on the love story of a young British man who travels to America and falls in love with an American girl, and how the social upheavals of the period impact their relationship and the lives of the people around them.

Aladdin (1992; rated G; 90 minutes). A Disney animated musical based on the folktale of Aladdin and the lamp. A young thief, tricked into working for the evil grand vizier to the kindly sultan, finds a magic lamp and frees the genie from within it. Aladdin uses his wishes to try to win the heart of the sultan's daughter and defeat the grand vizier.

Ali Baba Goes to Town (1937; not rated; 77 minutes). In search of a film star's autograph, a man has an accident while on the movie set for *Ali Baba* and injures his head, resulting in his dreaming himself into ancient Arabia. The film uses its fantasy setting to mock the economic policies of President Franklin D. Roosevelt.

Amadeus (1984; rated R; 160 minutes). A fictionalized biography of the life of Wolfgang Amadeus Mozart as told by his rival, Antonio Salieri.

An American in Paris (1951; not rated; 113 minutes). A former American GI is living in post–World War II Paris in the hopes of becoming a painter.

Annie (1982; rated PG; 127 minutes). In 1930s New York City, a young orphan named Annie is allowed to live in the house of the wealthy Daddy Warbucks as a publicity stunt to improve his image. Annie charms everyone she meets, including President Roosevelt, and is adopted by Warbucks. (In 2014 the film was remade and set in the early 2000s.)

Annie Get Your Gun (1950; not rated; 107 minutes). The backwoods Annie Oakley becomes the sharp-shooting star of Buffalo Bill's famous Wild West Show. She first competes, and then falls in love, with fellow performer Frank Butler.

The Band Wagon (1953; not rated; 112 minutes). A movie star in a slump agrees to star in a Broadway musical—*The Band Wagon*—coauthored by his friends. The musical's director decides to cast a ballerina in the show and to reimagine the musical comedy as high art. The movie star and the ballerina fall in love and save the show by going back to its original comedic concept.

Beach Blanket Bingo (1965; not rated; 98 minutes). A convoluted plot involving a singer, skydiving stunts, bikers, a kidnapping scheme, and a man falling in love with a mermaid.

Beauty and the Beast (1991; rated G; 84 minutes). A Disney animated musical based on the fairy tale by the same name. A young, bookish woman named Belle goes to the castle of the Beast to save her father. Belle and the Beast slowly fall in love, and through love the Beast is transformed back into a young man.

Bells Are Ringing (1960; not rated; 126 minutes). A young woman works for a telephone answering service, taking messages for people when they are unavailable. Through her work, she becomes involved in the lives of the people she only knows over the phone and falls in love with one of her clients. Meanwhile, local gangsters use the answering service as a front for their gambling operation.

Billy Elliot (2000; rated R; 110 minutes). Set in 1984, a young boy being raised by his father in northern England coal-mining country wants to become a professional ballet dancer. Though Billy is truly talented, his father is appalled at the idea of his son being a dancer.

The Boy Friend (1971; rated G; 257 minutes). A complex homage to, and satire of, film musicals. The framing story is set in 1920s England, where a theatrical troupe is performing a musical; a film producer happens to be in the audience. The musical being performed involves four British schoolgirls in the South of France and features musical fantasy sequences dreamed by the characters performing in the musical.

The Broadway Melody (1929; not rated; 100 minutes). Two sisters try to succeed on Broadway, and both are in love with the same man. In the end, the younger sister marries and leaves show business, while the elder sister continues with her career but is clearly lonely.

The Bronze Buckaroo (1939; not rated; 58 minutes). Cowboy Bob Blake and his friends attempt to solve the mystery of their friend, Joe, who disappeared from his Texas ranch (it is later revealed that the ranch sits on a gold mine). A rival had kidnapped Joe who tries to force him to sign over the deed to his ranch, but his friends rescue him.

Bye Bye Birdie (1963; rated G; 112 minutes). Rock star Conrad Birdie is drafted, devastating his teenage girl fans. Struggling songwriter Albert is devastated too because now Birdie will not be able to record his song, but Albert's girlfriend schemes to have Birdie sing one last time to a randomly selected fan on *The Ed Sullivan Show*.

Cabaret (1972; rated PG; 122 minutes). A love triangle between an American female cabaret singer, a British scholar, and an aristocratic German playboy unfolds in 1931 Berlin with the rise of the Nazi Party as backdrop.

Cabin in the Sky (1943; not rated; 98 minutes). An all-black musical featuring Ethel Waters as the long-suffering wife of Joe, compulsive gambler. Unknown to them, an angel and the son of the devil are fighting for the right to Joe's soul.

Camelot (1967; rated G; 179 minutes). Framed as a flashback to explain why best friends King Arthur and Sir Lancelot are set to do battle, the plot traces out both the establishment of the Knights of the Round Table and the democratic ideal it represents, as well as the love triangle between King Arthur, his wife Guinevere, and Sir Lancelot that ultimately destroys it.

Can't Help Singing (1944; not rated; 90 minutes). A senator's daughter follows her boyfriend out to California during the gold rush, but on her way there she falls in love with someone else.

Carmen Jones (1954; not rated; 105 minutes). An adaptation of Bizet's opera *Carmen*, this all-black musical is set during World War II at a parachute factory.

Carousel (1956; not rated; 126 minutes). Set in late nineteenth-century Maine, a carnival barker, Billy Bigelow, falls in love and marries a local mill girl, and they both lose their jobs. Billy is killed attempting a robbery in order to support his pregnant wife; an angel sends him back to earth for a chance at redemption.

Chicago (2002; rated PG-13; 113 minutes). Two murderous women compete for fame and stardom in 1920s Chicago. The film satirizes celebrity culture and the legal system.

Chitty Chitty Bang Bang (1968; rated G; 144 minutes). The two children of an eccentric inventor attempt to bring their widowed father together with the beautiful daughter of a candy maker. While the quartet is at the beach together, the father tells everyone a fantasy story about an evil baron who attempts to steal his latest invention, a flying car.

The Commitments (1991; rated R; 118 minutes). In Northern Ireland, a working-class man forms a tribute band to American soul music.

The Congress Dances (1932; not rated; 83 minutes). Diplomacy and romance take place during the 1814 Congress of Vienna, as various European powers attempt to address the end of the Napoleonic Wars.

A Connecticut Yankee in King Arthur's Court (1949; not rated; 106 minutes). In this loose adaptation of Mark Twain's novel of the same name, star Bing Crosby is hit on the head in 1912, imagines himself back in the time of King Arthur, and gains power and influence thanks to his modern-day knowledge.

The Court Jester (1955; not rated; 101 minutes). A carnival performer and a maid are charged with protecting a baby who is the rightful royal heir to the throne.

De-Lovely (2004; rated PG-13; 125 minutes). A biography of the composer Cole Porter.

Doctor Dolittle (1967; rated G; 152 minutes). In Victorian England, Dr. Dolittle is an expert at treating his animal patients because he can talk to them, but he is much less successful at interacting with human beings.

Don't Play Us Cheap (1973; not rated; 141 minutes). A bored pair of devils decides to cause trouble at a Harlem house party, but one of them ends up falling in love.

Down Argentine Way (1940; not rated; 89 minutes). A young man travels from Argentina to New York in order to sell horses and falls in love with the niece of the man who cheated his father in a business deal. Later, the two meet again in Argentina and after a horse race persuade the father to allow them to marry.

Dreamgirls (2006; rated PG-13; 130 minutes). An all-girl, all-black music trio in 1960s Detroit finds national success at the expense of one of its members.

8 Mile (2002; rated R; 110 minutes). Set in the mid-1990s, a young, working-class white man from Detroit uses his ability to rap in order to find personal success.

The Emperor's New Groove (2002; rated G; 78 minutes). A Disney animated musical about a selfish Inca leader who is turned into a llama by his evil advisor, and who tries to regain his throne (and his human form) with the help of a peasant.

Evergreen (1934; not rated; 94 minutes). Set in Edwardian England, a popular singing star hides the fact that she has an illegitimate daughter. Blackmailed from the stage, she flees to South Africa; years later her grown-up daughter returns to London hoping to become a star.

Evita (1996; rated PG; 135 minutes). Beginning with the death of protagonist Eva "Evita" Peron in 1952, the film depicts the rise and fall of the wife of Argentine president Juan Peron.

Fame (1980; rated R; 134 minutes). An episodic film covering the lives of a group of students at the New York High School of Performing Arts from their auditions through their senior year.

Fiddler on the Roof (1971; rated G; 181 minutes). The story of the Tevye family, an Orthodox Jewish family in Russia during the early 1900s.

Flower Drum Song (1961; not rated; 133 minutes). A Chinese woman and her father who illegally immigrate to Chinatown, Los Angeles, meet and are helped by a local Chinese American family who are dealing with intergenerational conflict and the tensions between being "Chinese" and being "American."

Footloose (1984; rated PG; 107 minutes). A young man from Chicago finds himself in a small town that has banned dancing after a group of students were killed in a car crash coming home from a school dance. He falls in love with the daughter of the local reverend and tries to persuade the town to lift their ban.

For Me and My Gal (1942; not rated; 104 minutes). On the eve of World War I, a vaudeville performer first attempts to avoid the draft, volunteers for the war effort after his girlfriend leaves him for doing so, and becomes a war hero.

42nd Street (1933; not rated; 89 minutes). In the middle of the Great Depression, a director and two producers attempt to stage a new Broadway musical with an aging, and demanding, actress. When the star is injured, a talented newcomer from the chorus is made into a star. The impact of the Great Depression is felt throughout the film.

Frozen (2013; rated PG; 102 minutes). An animated Disney musical loosely based on *The Snow Queen*, two sisters (and princesses)—Anna and Elsa—become estranged when Elsa cannot control her power to freeze things, especially when her emotions are triggered.

Funny Face (1957; not rated; 103 minutes). A fashion photographer accidentally takes the picture of an employee of a bookstore. Her "look" is so unique that he believes she could be a successful model; while in Paris the two fall in love.

Funny Girl (1968; rated G; 103 minutes). A musical biography of comedienne Fanny Brice (1891–1951).

A Funny Thing Happened on the Way to the Forum (1966; not rated; 99 minutes). A Roman slave attempts to obtain his freedom by playing matchmaker for his master's son.

Gigi (1958; not rated; 155 minutes). In turn-of-the-twentieth-century Paris, fifteen-year-old Gigi matures into a woman, and the older playboy who thought of her as a little sister falls in love with her.

Gold Diggers of 1933 (1933; not rated; 97 minutes). Broadway showgirl Polly does not know that her aspiring songwriter boyfriend is actually the heir to a fortune trying to make his way on the strength of his talent rather than his name. His family presumes that Polly is a gold digger, but ultimately the two are able to marry.

The Golden Dawn (1930; not rated; 83 minutes). Set in Africa during World War I, a white woman raised to believe she is African falls in love with a British soldier.

The Good Companions (1933; not rated; 95 minutes). An unlikely group of Britons come together with a theatrical troupe, name themselves "The Good Companions," and start to find success.

The Great American Broadcast (1941; not rated; 90 minutes). A few years after World War I, two friends go into the radio broadcasting business, fall out over their love for the same woman, and succeed in making the first coast-to-coast radio broadcast.

Hair (1979; rated PG; 121 minutes). Set in America during the Vietnam War, this is a story of a group of hippies.

Hairspray (2007; rated PG; 117 minutes). A young white girl in 1960s Baltimore decides to integrate her local television dance show.

Hallelujah (1929; not rated; 109 minutes). An all-black musical about a sharecropper who becomes a minister, marries a woman who is wrong for him, and kills the man with whom she is having an affair. The film ends with his release from prison and redemption.

Hallelujah, I'm a Bum (1933; not rated; 82 minutes). A hobo in New York during the Great Depression—known as the "mayor" of Central Park—prevents a young woman from committing suicide.

The Harvey Girls (1946; not rated; 104 minutes). Beginning in 1870, Fred Harvey built a chain of railway hotels and restaurants across the Southwest, most built alongside railroads. Women from all over the country were hired as waitresses—symbols of eastern refinement in the heart of the frontier. One such Harvey girl journeys west to find a husband, only to become a spirited leader in the Harvey girls' feud with the men of the Alhambra Saloon.

Hello Dolly! (1969; rated G; 146 minutes). In 1890s New York, a widow named Dolly is a matchmaker. Her latest client is a grumpy rich man with whom she has fallen in love; he wants to marry the owner of a hat shop. Dolly arranges things so that everyone winds up romantically partnered with the right person.

Help! (1965; not rated; 92 minutes). The drummer for the Beatles, Ringo, possesses a ring sent to him by a female fan; the fan is slated to be sacrificed by an Eastern cult, but she must be wearing the ring for the sacrifice to work. Members of the cult track down Ringo, who cannot remove the ring from his finger, and a series of chases ensue.

Hercules (1997; rated G; 93 minutes). An animated Disney musical. Hercules, the infant son of the Greek gods Zeus and Hera, is stripped of his powers by Hades and raised by humans. When Hercules learns of his true parentage, he also discovers that he can only regain his powers by becoming a "true hero."

High School Musical (2006; rated G; 98 minutes). They are two high school students from different social worlds—he is a basketball player, she is a geek—but they both love singing. They become friends, become involved in a high school musical, fall in love, and undermine the social hierarchy of the school along the way.

Hipsters (2008; not rated; 120 minutes). In 1950s Soviet Russia a group of young people emulate American music and form a counterculture as a form of rebellion.

Hollywood Canteen (1944; not rated; 124 minutes). Two soldiers during World War II are sent to Hollywood to recover from their injuries before being sent back to the front. They go to the Hollywood Canteen, where soldiers can eat for free and see the stars perform.

How to Succeed in Business without Really Trying (1967; not rated; 121 minutes). A window cleaner becomes a business tycoon by following the advice in a book.

The Hunchback of Notre Dame (1996; rated G; 91 minutes). A Disney animated musical based on the Victor Hugo book of the same name, with the addition of three talking, comedic gargoyles who are Quasimodo's friends.

Idlewild (2006; rated R; 121 minutes). An all-black musical set in the 1930s American South. Two childhood friends grow up to be two very different people. One is shy but an amazing musician; the other is brash and the owner of a nightclub.

Into the Woods (2014; rated PG; 124 minutes). An interweaving of the characters and their stories from various fairy tales—including Jack and the Beanstalk, Cinderella, Little Red Riding Hood, and Rapunzel—and what happens to the various characters as they interact.

Jailhouse Rock (1957; not rated; 96 minutes). A man is imprisoned for killing someone in a bar fight, is mentored in music by his cellmate, and finds fame as a musician after his release from prison.

The Jazz Singer (1927; not rated; 96 minutes). Set in 1920 New York City, the son of a cantor becomes a performer (in blackface) and changes his name to hide his Jewish identity. Eventually he reclaims his identity and his family accepts his calling as a performer.

Jupiter's Darling (1955; not rated; 95 minutes). Set in Ancient Rome, Hannibal is ready to conquer the city but is prevented from doing so when he falls in love with a Roman woman.

The King and I (1956; not rated; 133 minutes). In the mid-1860s, a widowed English governess goes to Siam to teach the King's many wives and children.

Kismet (1955; not rated; 103 minutes). Set in Baghdad's distant past, a poor poet is kidnapped when he is mistaken for the man who cursed a notorious thief, setting off a chain of events that involve the poet's daughter, a caliph pretending to be a commoner, and a scheming wazir.

Lady Sings the Blues (1972; rated R; 144 minutes). A musical biography of the singer Billie Holiday, starring Diana Ross.

Lagaan (2001; rated PG; 234 minutes). In 1890s British India, suffering from a drought and newly imposed tax, a group of Indian villagers engage a game of cricket. If the villagers win, they will not need to pay taxes for three years. If they lose, they will owe the British three times their normal taxes.

Les Miserables (2012; rated PG-13; 158 minutes). Based on the novel by Victor Hugo, the film is set after the French Revolution and follows the story of petty thief Jean Valjean who breaks parole and is relentlessly pursued by the policeman Officer Javert.

Li'l Abner (1959; not rated; 114 minutes). A movie based on a satirical comic strip. The town of Dogpatch, U.S.A., will become a nuclear testing site unless its citizens can prove the value of the town to the government.

The Lion King (1994; not rated; 88 minutes). A Disney animated musical about a young lion who must take his place as king of beasts after his evil uncle kills his father.

The Little Mermaid (1989; rated G; 83 minutes). A Disney animated musical that adapts the Hans Christian Andersen story of the same name. A young mermaid falls in love with a prince and makes a deal with a sea witch to lose her tail and gain legs in order to woo the prince.

The Littlest Rebel (1935; rated PG; 70 minutes). Set in the American South at the beginning of the Civil War, a little girl's father becomes a scout for the Confederate Army.

Man of La Mancha (1972; rated PG; 132 minutes). Set during the Spanish Inquisition, the novelist Miguel de Cervantes and his servant are imprisoned for crimes against the Catholic Church. While in prison, they act out the story of Don Quixote, an old man who believes himself to be a knight.

Meet Me in St. Louis (1944; not rated; 112 minutes). A year in the life of a St. Louis family just prior to the 1904 World's Fair.

Moulin Rouge! (2001; rated PG-13; 128 minutes). At the turn of the twentieth century, a young British writer comes to Paris to pursue his dreams, befriends a group of Bohemians who are trying to write a musical entitled *Spectacular Spectacular*, and falls in love with a nightclub singer/courtesan who is dying from tuberculosis.

Mulan (1998; rated G; 87 minutes). A Disney animated musical based on a Chinese folktale. A young woman disguises herself as a man to fight in the Chinese army in the place of her father.

The Music Man (1962; not rated; 151 minutes). In a fictional Iowa city during the 1910s, a traveling salesman decides to con the entire town into paying him to form an all-boys marching band. But as he works to sell the townspeople on his idea, he falls in love with the local librarian.

My Fair Lady (1964; rated G; 170 minutes). In Edwardian England, where a person's accent marks them as high born or as low class, a phonetics scholar bets his friend that he can train a Cockney flower girl to speak as well as any duchess and thus fit in within high London society.

Naughty Marietta (1935; rated G; 105 minutes). In eighteenth-century France, a young woman does not want to marry the man selected for her by the king; she flees to the colony of Louisiana in the guise of her maid, Marietta, and is labeled a fugitive by the French government. She meets and falls in love with an American, and ultimately the two must flee from New Orleans for the wilderness so that they can be together.

Newsies (1992; rated PG; 121 minutes). Set in New York City, the movie is based on the newspaper-delivery-boy strike of 1899, triggered by a rise in distribution costs that the boys could not afford.

Oh! What a Lovely War (1969; rated G; 144 minutes). A British perspective, summary, and commentary on the events of World War I. Using songs from the period and dialogue based on primary sources, the film is also highly theatrical and stylized in its representation of the war.

Oklahoma! (1955; not rated; 145 minutes). Set in the early 1900s, before Oklahoma has become a state, a farmhand and a cowboy vie for the love of the same girl.

Oliver! (1968; rated G; 153 minutes). Based on the novel *Oliver Twist* by Charles Dickens, the movie tells the story of an innocent orphan boy in London who takes up with a gang of pickpockets.

On the Town (1949; not rated; 98 minutes). Three sailors on a twenty-four-hour shore leave in New York City each have different ideas of how they want to experience the city, but they all find romance along the way.

Paint Your Wagon (1969; rated PG-13; 154 minutes). Two gold prospectors in nineteenth-century California fall in love with the same woman, and she falls in love with both of them. But as the boomtown grows up around them, the trio needs to amend their relationship.

The Pajama Game (1957; not rated; 101 minutes). A new foreman, Sid, has been hired at an Iowa pajama factory, and the union employees—represented by Katherine "Babe" Williams—want a raise of seven and a half cents. As might be expected, romantic complications ensue.

Pocahontas (1995; rated G; 81 minutes). A Disney animated musical based on the encounter between British colonizers, led by Captain John Smith, and the Native Americans of Virginia in the seventeenth century.

The Producers (2005; rated PG; 134 minutes). A down-on-his-luck Broadway show producer partners with an accountant to produce a deliberately bad show about Hitler because a flop will earn them more money than a hit.

Rent (2005; rated PG-13; 135 minutes). The musical takes place over the course of one year in the lives of a group of young New Yorkers struggling to succeed in their various professions, with an emphasis on the ways in which the AIDS epidemic of the 1990s impacts their lives.

Road to Bali (1952; not rated; 91 minutes). Two American performers in Australia leave Melbourne in a hurry to avoid getting married and wind up as volunteer pearl divers near Bali, only to next find themselves shipwrecked and in love with the same woman.

The Road to Hong Kong (1962; not rated; 91 minutes). Two American con artists are in India when one is injured and loses his memory; the only cure is in Tibet. Along the way, they accidentally pick up a briefcase belonging to a spy and through a series of events wind up in a rocket ship to outer space.

Road to Singapore (1940; not rated; 85 minutes). Two men are determined to remain bachelors forever; they set off for Singapore when the father of one decides his son needs to settle down and get married.

Rose Marie (1936; not rated; 102 minutes). A Canadian opera singer in Montreal has a criminal brother who has recently escaped from prison, so she sets off into the wilderness to find him. Along the way she meets and falls in love with the Canadian Mountie determined to bring her brother to justice.

Saturday Night Fever (1977; rated R; 118 minutes). An Italian American working-class man in Brooklyn feels trapped by his job and his family; he only feels powerful and in control of his life when dancing at the disco.

Selena (1997; rated PG; 127 minutes). A biography of the Mexican American singer Selena Quintanilla, who was just starting to cross over into English-language markets when a disgruntled fan shot her to death in 1995.

Seven Brides for Seven Brothers (1954; rated G; 102 minutes). In 1850s Oregon, the oldest of seven brothers marries a woman, Millie, not out of love but to keep house for the family. The younger brothers decide that they want brides too and kidnap women from the town, but Millie makes sure that the brothers behave like gentlemen, and everyone eventually finds love.

1776 (1972; not rated; 141 minutes). The men who would become the signers of the Declaration of Independence come together in Philadelphia to debate whether or not to declare war on England. The film uses John Adams as its central protagonist and weaves primary source material throughout.

Shake, Rattle and Rock (1956; not rated; 72 minutes). A group of adults in an American city during the 1950s attempts to ban rock and roll because they are afraid the music will corrupt their teenagers; the fight cumulates in a televised trial over the value of rock music.

The Shocking Miss Pilgrim (1947; not rated; 85 minutes). In 1870s Boston, a woman typist goes to work for a shipping company and becomes involved in the suffrage movement.

Show Boat (1936 and 1951; not rated; 113 and 107 minutes). Life on a Mississippi River showboat from the 1880s through the 1920s. The young Magnolia falls in love and marries a riverboat gambler; the two later separate and then find their way back to one another. In a secondary plot, a light-skinned black woman on the showboat passes for white, but ultimately she cannot sustain the lie.

Silk Stockings (1957; not rated; 117 minutes). An American movie producer in Paris attempts to persuade a Soviet composer to write music for his films. In the meanwhile, Communist operatives—including a beautiful but cold woman—are sent to Paris to bring the composer back to Soviet Russia.

Singin' in the Rain (1952; not rated; 103 minutes). A comedic take on the transition in Hollywood from silent films to "talkies."

The Sound of Music (1965; rated G; 174 minutes). On the eve of World War II, a young novice in Austria becomes a nanny to the seven children of a widowed naval officer and falls in love.

South Pacific (1958; not rated; 171 minutes). At an army base on an island in the South Pacific during World War II, an American army nurse falls in love with an older French ex-patriot, but her upbringing makes it difficult for her to accept his mixed-race children from a previous relationship. In a parallel story, a navy lieutenant falls in love with a native woman.

Star-Spangled Rhythm (1942; not rated; 99 minutes). Set at the Paramount Studio during World War II, a former silent movie star tells his son, who is in the navy, that he is a studio executive (when in fact he is a security guard). When his son and sailor friends visit Paramount while on shore leave, a switchboard operator helps the dad persuade Paramount stars to put on a show for the sailors.

Stormy Weather (1943; not rated; 78 minutes). An all-black musical. Beginning in World War I, two struggling performers meet and fall in love but go their own ways in order to find fame. As the Second World War looms, they both grow famous but are unable to fully connect until fate brings them together one last time.

Summer Stock (1950; not rated; 109 minutes). Jane owns a struggling farm in Connecticut while supporting her sister's acting lessons in New York City. The sister unexpectedly brings an acting troupe to the farm so they can rehearse in the barn. While initially upset, Jane finds herself attracted both to the troupe's director and to the idea of acting.

Sunshine on Leith (2013; rated PG; 100 minutes). Using thirteen songs by the British band the Proclaimers, the film follows two Scottish soldiers who have returned to Edinburgh after serving a tour of duty in Afghanistan as they try to reclaim their old lives (and their girlfriends/wives).

Sweeney Todd: The Demon Barber of Fleet Street (2007; rated R; 116 minutes). Set in 1840s London, a barber called Sweeney Todd returns home many years after having been transported to Australia by a corrupt judge. With the help of a meat-pie shop owner, Mrs. Lovett, Todd wreaks revenge on those who wronged him, while Mrs. Lovett neatly disposes of the bodies.

The Sword in the Stone (1963; rated G; 79 minutes). A Disney animated film. The king of England, Uther Pendragon, dies without an heir, and a sword trapped in an anvil materializes in London. The person who pulls out the sword is the rightful king. It turns out that person is a boy nicknamed Wart, who, with the help of the wizard Merlin, will grow up to be King Arthur.

Tarzan (1999; rated G; 88 minutes). A Disney animated film. In the late 1880s, a British man, his wife, and their infant son are shipwrecked off the coast of Africa. After the husband and wife are killed, a female gorilla raises the infant as her own. Years later, a group of British explorers arrive and Tarzan must choose between life in Africa and a new life in England.

Thank Your Lucky Stars (1943; not rated; 124 minutes). Produced as a fundraiser for the war effort by the Warner Bros. Studio.

That Thing You Do! (1996; rated PG; 108 minutes). In 1960s Erie, Pennsylvania, the members of a local rock band produce a hit song and tour the country.

This Is the Army (1943; not rated; 121 minutes). The movie begins in World War I and ends in the middle of World War II. A theater performer returns home from the First World War, has a family, and sees his son enlist in the army during the Second World War.

Tommy (1975; rated PG; 108 minutes). A rock musical based on the concept album of the same name by the Who. A deaf, mute, and blind boy becomes a "pinball wizard," and a cult of followers grows up around him.

Top Hat (1935; not rated; 101 minutes). An American dancer in London is mistaken for a married man by a woman he meets in a hotel, and she decides to teach him a lesson for flirting when (apparently) married. Stars Fred Astaire and Ginger Rogers.

Tumbling Tumbleweeds (1935; not rated; 61 minutes). A singing cowboy returns home to the ranch after the murder of his father.

Up in Arms (1944; not rated; 106 minutes). A hypochondriac is drafted into the army during World War II and is sent to the Pacific theater.

We'll Meet Again (1942; not rated; 84 minutes). A young British dancer in London during World War II finds fame as a singer instead.

West Side Story (1961; rated PG; 152 minutes). A retelling of Romeo and Juliet, set in New York City with gangs—one comprised of whites, the other comprised of Puerto Ricans—substituted for the rival families in the original play.

Wild Style (1983; rated R; 82 minutes). A hip-hop musical set in the Bronx follows a young man who plays by the rules by day but is a graffiti artist by night.

The Wiz (1978; rated G; 134 minutes). An updated, all-black version of *The Wizard of Oz.*

The Wizard of Oz (1939; rated G; 101 minutes). A young farm girl from Kansas is transported to the magical Land of Oz, where she meets the Scarecrow, the Tin Man, and the Cowardly Lion. Together, they defeat the Wicked Witch of the West.

Yankee Doodle Dandy (1942; not rated; 126 minutes). A musical biography of the Broadway composer and playwright George M. Cohan.

Zoot Suit (1981; rated R; 103 minutes). A musical based on the Los Angeles Zoot Suit Riots that erupted in the 1940s between Mexican Americans and white American servicemen.

Further Reading

Altman, Rick. *The American Film Musical*. Bloomington: Indiana University Press, 1987.
Association of American Colleges and Universities. "Essential Learning Outcomes." Accessed October 14, 2016. http://www.aacu.org/.
Austin, Jake. *TV-a-Go-Go: Rock on TV from American Bandstand to American Idol*. Chicago: Chicago Review Press, 2005.
Babal, Marianne. "Sticky History: Connecting Historians with the Public." *Public Historian* 32, no. 4 (Fall 2010): 76–84.
Barrios, Richard. *Dangerous Rhythm: Why Movie Musicals Matter*. New York: Oxford University Press, 2014.
———. *A Song in the Dark*. New York: Oxford University Press, 1995.
Basinger, Jeanine. *A Woman's View: How Hollywood Spoke to Women, 1930–1960*. Middletown, CT: Wesleyan University Press, 1993.
———. *The World War II Combat Film: Anatomy of a Genre*. Middletown, CT: Wesleyan University Press, 2003.
Baskett, Michael. *The Attractive Empire: Transnational Film Culture in Imperial Japan*. Honolulu: University of Hawaii Press, 2008.
Beck, Jerry. "The Little Mermaid." In *The Animated Movie Guide*, 147–48. Chicago: Chicago Review Press, 2005.
Bergfelder, Tim, Sue Harris, and Sarah Street. *Film Architecture and the Transnational Imagination: Set Design in 1930s European Cinema*. Amsterdam: Amsterdam University Press, 2007.
Beumers, Birgit. "Soviet and Russian Blockbusters: A Question of Genre?" *Slavic Review* 6, no. 3 (Autumn 2003): 441–54.
Blight, David W. "'For Something beyond the Battlefield': Frederick Douglass and the Struggle for the Memory of the Civil War." *Journal of American History* 75, no. 4 (March 1989): 1156–78.
Brah, Avtar, and Ann Phoenix. "Ain't I a Woman? Revisiting Intersectionality." *Journal of International Women's Studies* 5, no. 3 (May 2004): 75–86. http://vc.bridgew.edu/.
Calloway, Colin, ed. *Dawnland Encounters: Indians and Europeans in Northern New England*. Hanover, NH: University Press of New England, 1991.
Chandler, Daniel. "An Introduction to Genre Theory." Kubrick Site, August 11, 1997. http://visual-memory.co.uk/.
Desai, Jigna, and Rajinder Dudrah. "The Essential Bollywood." In *The Bollywood Reader*, edited by Rajinder Dudrah and Jigna Desai, 1–18. Maidenhead, UK: McGraw-Hill Education, 2008.

Douglass, Frederick. "Decoration Day: A Verbatim Report of the Address of Frederick Douglass at Franklin Square, Rochester, N.Y." 1871. Frederick Douglass Papers, Speech, Article, and Book File, Library of Congress. http://www.loc.gov/.

Dyer, Richard. "Entertainment and Utopia." In *Only Entertainment*, 19–35. New York: Routledge, 1999.

———. "Is *Car Wash* a Musical?" In *Black American Cinema*, edited by Manthia Diawara, 93–106. New York: Routledge, 1993.

Faulkner, Sally. *A History of Spanish Film: Cinema and Society, 1910–2010*. London: Bloomsbury, 2013.

Feuer, Jane. *The Hollywood Musical*. Bloomington: Indiana University Press, 1993.

———. "Hollywood Musicals: Mass Art as Folk Art." *Jump Cut* (October 1980): 23–25.

———. "The Self-Reflexive Musical and the Myth of Entertainment." In *Film Genre Reader II*, edited by Barry Keith Grant, 441–55. Austin: University of Texas Press, 1995.

Fordin, Hugh. *M-G-M's Greatest Musicals: The Arthur Freed Unit*. New York: De Capo, 1975.

Gehlawat, Ajay. *Reframing Bollywood: Theories of Popular Hindi Cinema*. Washington, DC: Sage, 2010.

Ginzburg, Carlo. "Microhistory: Two or Three Things That I Know about It." In *Threads and Traces*, translated by Anne C. Tedeschi and John Tedeschi, 193–214. Berkeley: University of California Press, 2012.

Grant, Barry Keith. *The Hollywood Film Musical*. Malden, MA: Wiley-Blackwell, 2012.

Gunning, Tom. "The Whole Town's Gawking: Early Cinema and the Visual Experience of Modernity." *Yale Journal of Criticism* 7, no. 2 (1994): 189–201.

Hollitz, John. "The Truth about Textbooks." In *Thinking through the Past: A Critical Thinking Approach to U.S. History*. Vol. 1: *To 1877*, 7–20. 4th ed. Boston: Wadsworth Cengage Learning, 2010.

Horn, Barbara Lee. *The Age of Hair: Evolution and Impact of Broadway's First Rock Musical*. Westwood, CT: Greenwood, 1991.

Humanities Blast. "The Digital Humanities Manifesto 2.0." Accessed October 14, 2016. http://www.humanitiesblast.com/.

James, David E. *Rock 'n' Film: Cinema's Dance with Popular Music*. Oxford: Oxford University Press, 2015.

John, Anthony. "Song and Audience in Early Film Musicals." *American Music Research Center Journal* 11 (2001): 35–45.

Joyner, Charles. *Shared Traditions: Southern History and Folk Culture*. Urbana: University of Illinois Press, 1999.

Katsnelson, Anna Wexler. "The Tramp in a Skirt: Laboring the Radiant Path." *Slavic Review* 70, no. 2 (Summer 2011): 256–78.

Kelley, Robin D. G. "'But a Local Phase of a World Problem': Black History's Global Vision, 1883–1950." *Journal of American History* 86, no. 3 (1999): 1045–77.

Kennedy, Matthew. *Roadshow! The Fall of Film Musicals in the 1960s*. New York: Oxford University Press, 2014.

Larsen, Dale. *A Book about the Film* Monty Python and the Holy Grail*: All the References from African Swallows to Zoot*. Lanham, MD: Rowman & Littlefield, 2015.

Laville, Helen. "'Our Country Endangered by Underwear': Fashion, Femininity, and the Seduction Narrative in *Ninotchka* and *Silk Stockings*." *Diplomatic History* 30, no. 4 (September 2006): 623–44.

Lawrence, Michael. "India." In *The International Film Musical*, edited by Corey Creekmur and Linda Mokdad, 189–210. Edinburgh: Edinburgh University Press, 2012.

"The Little Mermaid." In "Disney Theatrical Animated Features: The Complete Guide," edited by Paul Muljadi. *Wikipedia*, 2011. http://www.wikiwand.com/.

Lott, Tommy. "Hollywood and Independent Black Cinema." In *Contemporary Hollywood Cinema*, edited by Steve Neale and Murray Smith, 211–28. New York: Routledge, 1998.

Majumdar, Neepa. *Wanted: Cultured Ladies Only! Female Stardom and Cinema in India, 1930s–1950s*. Urbana: University of Illinois Press, 2009.

Marcus, Alan S., Scott Alan Metzger, Richard J. Paxton, and Jeremy D. Stoddard. *Teaching History with Film: Strategies for Secondary Social Studies*. New York: Routledge, 2010.

Mast, Gerald. *Can't Help Singin'*. New York: Overlook, 1987.

McMillin, Scott. *The Musical as Drama*. Princeton, NJ: Princeton University Press, 2014.

Miller, Marc. "Of Tunes and Toons: The Movie Musical in the 1990s." In *Film Genre 2000: New Critical Essays*, edited by Wheeler W. Dixon. Albany: SUNY Press, 2000.

Monteyne, Kimberly. *Hip Hop on Film: Performance Culture, Urban Space, and Genre Transformation*. Jackson: University Press of Mississippi, 2013.

Mulvey, Laura. "Visual Pleasure and Narrative Cinema." *Screen* 16, no. 3 (Autumn 1975): 6–18.

Mundy, John. "Britain." In *The International Film Musical*, edited by Corey Creekmur and Linda Mokdad, 15–28. Edinburgh: Edinburgh University Press, 2012.

National Council on Public History. "About the Field: How Do We Define Public History?" Accessed October 14, 2016. http://ncph.org/.

Neale, Steve. *Genre*. London: British Film Institute, 1980.

Noroford, Bjorn. "The Post-Modern Transnational Film Musical." In *The International Film Musical*, edited by Corey Creekmur and Linda Mokdad, 241–56. Edinburgh: Edinburgh University Press, 2012.

Ostrow, Stuart. *Present at the Creation, Leaping in the Dark, and Going against the Grain*. New York: Applause Books, 2006.

Prokhorov, Alexander. "Cinema of Attractions versus Narrative Cinema: Leonid Gaidai's Comedies and El'dar Riazanov's Satires of the 1960s." *Slavic Review* 62, no. 3 (Autumn 2003): 455–72.

Rentschler, Eric. *The Use and Abuse of Cinema: German Legacies from the Weimar Era to the Present*. New York: Columbia University Press, 2015.

Rimgaila, Salys. *The Strange Afterlife of Stalinist Musical Films*. Washington, DC: National Council for Eurasian and East European Research, 2006. https://www.ucis.pitt.edu/nceeer/2003-817-08-Salys.pdf

Roy Rosenzweig Center for History in New Media. "Teaching Materials." 2014. Accessed October 14, 2016. http://chnm.gmu.edu/.

Schatz, Thomas. *Boom and Bust: American Cinema in the 1940s*. Berkeley: University of California Press, 1999.

Seckler, Dawn. "Genre Issues: What Does Zhanr Mean in Russian?" In *Directory of World Cinema: Russia*, edited by Birgit Beumers, 28–33. Chicago: Intellect Press, 2011.

Stanfield, Peter. *Horse Opera: The Strange History of the 1930s Singing Cowboy*. Urbana: University of Illinois Press, 2002.

Steven, Peter. "*Saturday Night Fever*: Just Dancing." *Jump Cut* 23 (October 1980): 13–16. http://www.ejumpcut.org/.

Stojanova, Christina. "New Russian Cinema." *Kinema* (Fall 1998): http://www.kinema.uwaterloo.ca/.

Taylor, Ella. "In Soviet Russia, Communism Can't Stop the Beat." NPR, February 23, 2012. http://www.npr.org/.

Taylor, Richard. "But Eastward, Look, the Land Is Brighter: Towards a Topography of Utopia in the Stalinist Musical." In *100 Years of European Cinema: Entertainment or Ideology?* edited by Diana Holmes and Alison Smith, 11–26. Manchester, UK: Manchester University Press, 2000.

Terenzio, Maurice, Scott MacGillivray, and Ted Okuda. *The Soundies Distributing Corporation of America*. Jefferson, NC: McFarland, 1991.

Tosh, John. "History Goes Public." In *Why History Matters*. New York: Palgrave Macmillan, 2008.

Townsend, Robert. *History's Babel: Scholarship, Professionalization, and the Historical Enterprise in the United States, 1880–1940*. Chicago: University of Chicago Press, 2013.

Villon, Francois. *Poems*. Translated by David Georgi. Evanston, IL: Northwestern University Press, 2013.

Walkerdine, Valerie. *Daddy's Girl: Young Girls and Popular Culture*. Cambridge, MA: Harvard University Press, 1998.

White, Hayden. "The Historical Text as Literary Artifact." In *Tropics of Discourse: Essays in Cultural Criticism*, 81–100. Baltimore: Johns Hopkins University Press, 1985.

Williams, Justin. *Rhymin' and Stealin': Musical Borrowing in Hip-Hop*. Ann Arbor: University of Michigan Press, 2014.

Williams, Linda. *Hard Core: Power, Pleasure, and the "Frenzy of the Visible."* Berkeley: University of California Press, 1999.

Youngblood, Denise J. "The Fate of Soviet Popular Cinema during the Stalin Revolution." *Russian Review* 50, no. 2 (April 1991): 148–62.

Zemon Davis, Natalie. *The Return of Martin Guerre*. Cambridge, MA: Harvard University Press, 1983.

Index

Civil War, 31, 35–36, 39, 47, 48–49, 52, 61, 66, 85, 118
Cold War, 60, 88, 91, 93, 94
collaboration, 7, 30–31, 32–33, 34, 49
The Congress Dances, 83, 114
Congress of Vienna, 83, 114
A Connecticut Yankee in King Arthur's Court, 57, 76, 77, 114

dance, ix, x, xi, 3, 5, 7, 9, 14, 15–16, 17, 39, 43, 52, 59, 62, 64–65, 66, 68, 88, 89, 93, 112, 115, 116, 122
Declaration of Independence, 26, 31–32, 47, 120
digital humanities, 23, 25, 33–34, 35
discussion starters, 5, 24, 44, 73
Doctor Dolittle, 12, 114
Donen, Stanley, 9
Don't Look Back, 13
Don't Play Us Cheap, 64, 65, 114
Down Argentine Way, 72, 114
Dreamgirls, 18, 114

Eddy, Nelson, 7, 88
Edwards, Sherman, 32
eighteenth century, 26, 31, 48, 81, 82, 119
England, xi, 31, 47, 63, 76–77, 80, 86, 93–94, 112, 114, 119, 120, 122
Enlightenment, 72, 81, 82
ethnicity, xii–xiii, 5, 44, 54, 56, 64, 67, 68, 69, 72, 88
Europe, xi, 11, 12, 46, 53, 55, 58, 59, 72, 77, 78, 79, 81, 82, 83, 84, 85, 86, 87, 88, 89–90, 91–92, 93, 94, 114
evidence, 23, 24, 28, 29, 64, 71, 74, 75, 76, 79, 84, 85, 91
Evita, 17, 115

Fame, 15, 115
Fiddler on the Roof, 87, 88, 89, 115
film musicals: adapted from stage musicals, 12–13, 18, 51, 52, 54, 59, 62, 65, 68, 76, 79, 83, 90; as genre, ix–x, xi, xiii, 3–4, 5, 6, 8, 9, 10, 11, 12–13, 14, 15, 16, 17–18, 19, 25, 33, 37, 43, 50, 60, 65, 67, 72, 90; fantasy in, xi, 3, 7, 15, 65, 111, 112; technology and, 8, 10, 25, 34, 50, 55; utopian elements, ix, 11, 14, 56, 64, 90

film musicals, types of: "all-black", 5, 6, 9, 15, 16, 37, 38, 55, 66, 113, 114, 116, 117, 121, 123; animated, 7, 16, 17, 18, 45, 84, 111, 112, 115, 117, 118, 119, 120, 122; backstage, xi, 3, 6, 7, 8, 9, 11, 13, 17, 18, 57, 58, 68; beach, 13, 62, 112; "Bollywood", 18; canteen, 8; concert, 13, 27; cowboy, 4, 8, 9, 113, 122; folk, 3, 6, 8; hip hop, 16, 36, 66–67, 123; made-for-television, 19; *Road*, 9; operetta, 7, 11, 16, 79, 83; teen, 13, 15, 67, 91
film studios: 20th Century Fox, 9; Disney, 7, 16, 18, 19, 45, 84; International Pictures, 13; MGM, 6, 7, 8, 9, 10–11, 16, 17, 75; RKO, 7, 8; Paramount, 9, 10, 16, 121; Warner Brothers, 6–7, 8, 122
Flower Drum Song, xii–xiii, 13, 115
folk music, 48, 55
Footloose, 15, 115
For Me and My Gal, 53, 115
founding fathers, 31, 46, 47
France, 18, 53, 58, 76, 79, 80, 83, 84, 85, 86, 112, 119
Franklin, Benjamin, x, 31
Freed Unit, 4, 8, 9, 10
French Revolution, 79, 84, 85, 88
Frozen, 7, 115
Funicello, Annette, 4, 13
Funny Face, 11, 115
A Funny Thing Happened on the Way to the Forum, 76, 115

Garland, Judy, 9, 53
gay/lesbian, 9, 67
gender, xi, xii, xiii, 5, 11, 14, 29, 45, 49–51, 54, 58, 59, 62, 65, 68, 69, 77, 92
Germany, 14, 91
Gigi, 11, 16, 23, 24, 28, 29, 115
The Golden Dawn, 90, 116
Goldiggers of 1933, 14, 67
The Great American Broadcast, 53, 116
Great Depression, 6, 9, 14, 35, 54, 55, 56, 57, 64, 115, 116
Great Migration, 38, 52, 53, 56
Gunning, Tom, ix

Hagen, Jean, 34

About the Author

Kathryn Edney is assistant professor of history at Regis College, where she teaches courses in U.S. history, historiography, and culture and society. Her writing has appeared in *Brecht, Broadway and United States Theater* (2007); *Sounds of the Future: Essays on Music in Science Fiction Film* (2010); *Movies, Music, and More: Advancing Popular Culture in the Writing Classroom* (2011); and *The Journal of Popular Culture.*

CPSIA information can be obtained
at www.ICGtesting.com
Printed in the USA
FSHW011252230919
62295FS